*Self-*Editing Essentials *for Nonfiction*

Revising organization, content, and writing

Katie Chambers

Beacon Point LLC

For permission requests, contact:
kmchambers@beaconpointservices.org.

ISBN: 979-8-9943102-2-9

Edited by Robin Samuels of Shadowcat Editing
Cover design by Karolina Wudniak of Paperwing Studio
Interior design by Liz Schreiter

Library of Congress Catalog Number: 2026905072
First printing: 2026
www.beaconpointservices.org

To my husband, Gary Chambers:

It might be cliché to dedicate a book to a spouse, but hear me out.
In my culture, people marry young, so by twenty-five I was already
considered an "old maid." Gary swept me up right as I turned thirty,
saving me from that perilous stage.

What he got in return was a woman who lives and breathes her work.
Not working would feel like cutting off my right arm. Through building
my company, raising three kids, and writing this book while scaling my
business, he has stood by me—even when that meant evenings alone
while I disappeared into my office after we had put the kids to bed.

None of this would be possible without his support and unwavering
belief in my abilities. So, yes, I'm dedicating this book to him.

Acknowledgements

Writing a book is no joke, and doing it alone would be impossible. Many people contributed to this book, more than I can list here.

EDITING CLIENTS

Thank you for trusting me with your manuscripts. I've grown as an editor through your books. Your books gave me the skills and perspective that built the foundation for this book.

LAUNCH TEAM MEMBERS

Too many to name here, but they were my champions and supporters throughout my entire journey.

BETA READERS

When my beta readers first encountered this project as a simple PDF, they saw its potential and pushed me to expand it into the book you're holding now.

James Gibbons, an incredible writer and poet who started writing at age five and now works as a copywriter.

Adrienne Pond, a fellow former teacher, now a nonfiction and fiction editor, writing coach, and writer of short fiction, essays, and memoirs.

Jackie Raymond, a nonfiction editor who shapes flabby writing into powerful prose and an aspiring nonfiction author.

Geo Maria Bughani, a nonfiction writer for the past 12 years (since 2014), writing for brands and ghostwriting for founders on LinkedIn.

Beth Bevis Gallick, a nonfiction writer and editor who has worked in publishing, academia, and the nonprofit sector.
Ross B Lampert, a published author who went above and beyond and gave me feedback line by line.

EDITOR

Even editors need editors. Thanks to Robin Samuels of Shadowcat Editing for her meticulous copyediting.

COVER AND INTERIOR BOOK DESIGNER

As someone with full aphantasia, I struggle with visual concepts, so I gave Karolina Wudniak of Paperwing Studio and Liz Schreiter very little to go on. I was basically like, "I don't know. Just make it look good." Well, the results speak for themselves.

Contents

The Professional Editing Roadmap—A 6-Step Educational Email Course

INTRODUCTION

So … you wrote a book. An actual book. That's freaking amazing!

Guess what? I wrote a book too.

You might be thinking, "Well, yes, Katie, I'm literally holding it." Fair. But I needed to say it out loud because I never imagined this would be me. I've helped nearly 300 books come to life (as of 2025!), but until now, I hadn't written one of my own.

Doing so challenged and intimidated me, and yet I did it anyway. And so did you!

Before we talk about fixing anything, pause and acknowledge that. Take a breath. Do a tiny celebration—strike a superhero pose, pump your fist, whisper "I'm awesome," eat a slice of pie, or dance in your kitchen. However you do it, mark the moment: You finished a book.

Okay, but now real talk. I have a hard truth that you may already know: Writing the book is only the beginning. Now you're stepping into the part that often feels overwhelming—editing and revising. Even though good writing is rewriting, this stage terrifies most writers. It excites me because I live here. But you're not me. I'm not going to sugarcoat it: Self-editing is hard work and takes time.

Still . . . remember what you've already done: You wrote an entire book, something big and difficult.

You can do this part too. The benefits are well worth the effort.

And I'll guide you through the process. As a former English teacher, teaching is at my core and influences how I edit. In every book I work on, I model specific types of edits in the text and explain why I made the changes I did so my authors feel empowered in their choices. This editing style prepared me well to write this book.

> If you need additional help, appendices A and B contain even more resources, and my inbox is always open: kmchambers@beaconpointservices.org.

Why learn to self-edit well

"Writing without revising is the literary equivalent of waltzing gaily out of the house in your underwear."

— PATRICIA FULLER —

So, revise and edit your manuscript yourself because no one wants to see your underwear.

You might be thinking, *Wait a second, I'll have clothes over my underwear. My draft will be revised and edited by an editor. Editors edit; writers write. I'll catch a few typos and grammar errors and then pay an editor to take care of the rest.*

Editors absolutely can take care of a lot, but you can't grow as a writer without editing your own work. According to a quote often attributed to Ernest Hemingway, "The only kind of writing is rewriting."

You need to put some basic clothes on over your underwear before an editor can work their fairy godperson magic and help turn those clothes into a dashing garment. If they have to start from your underwear, they can only take your book so far within the time and budget you have.

Putting on your own clothes, in this case, is hard work. Authors often say they spent more time revising than they did writing their initial draft. But if you skip this stage, your book will not be the best it could be.

In this guide, I'll walk you through an extensive self-editing process that includes multiple read-throughs. By adopting this process, you'll lessen the load of your editor—which *saves you money*—but more importantly, you'll

- end up with a better book
- challenge your writing brain
- learn your writing weaknesses

So while you technically can skip the self-editing, you really don't want to. And while AI can help you (I used it in my own self-editing for this book to flag wordy and unclear sentences and check for clarity), you still need to understand the basic principles of self-editing to guide any AI tool effectively. And even then, you shouldn't use just AI. Editing still requires a lot of human effort.

So long story short? The stronger your manuscript is when your editor gets it, the better your published book will be and the less money you'll spend on professional editing.

If you want more guided self-editing, check out my Manuscript Checkup services. I'll professionally edit your first 10k words and provide a one-on-one coaching call to teach you how to edit for the topics your manuscript needs most. After the call, I provide feedback on one self-edited chapter to help you apply the techniques with confidence (for more information, see appendix A).

Why do I need to hire an editor after thoroughly self-editing?

Self-editing is important, but self-editing alone won't bring your manuscript to its full potential. Even trained professional editors hire editors. I'm paying someone to edit mine. I know, I know. That's probably not what you wanted to hear. "Come on, Katie, after I do all this work myself, I still have to go hire someone?"

But you can never see your book from the reader's perspective because you wrote it so know too much. Now you need a pro who can provide that outside view. Plus, a good editor has undergone editorial training. You haven't (and no, this book doesn't qualify you as a professional editor).

If hiring a professional editor is not an option for you right now, though, don't let that stop you from pursuing your dream. You can go through this self-editing process more than once and enlist several beta readers to help strengthen your work. And if you publish without a professional edit, you can always invest your initial profits into hiring an editor down the road to revise and republish an updated second edition.

Preparing to self-edit

Before you begin this self-editing process, make sure you've got some distance from your manuscript. Wait a few weeks, or even months if needed, after you finish writing. Fresh eyes catch what tired ones miss.

Some writers like to read through their manuscript once and take notes before beginning their edits. Others dive straight in. Both work—pick whichever matches your brain.

> ### PAUSE HERE
>
> If you don't have enough distance from your first draft yet, put this book down and come back to it later.
>
> If you do have distance and you'd like to read through your manuscript before editing it, pause and do that now, then come back to this book to start the self-editing process.

How this guide is structured

This guide is designed to be used selectively, as a toolbox, not a linear nonfiction book. You'll get the most value by choosing to read what you need, when you need it.

EDITING PASSES

I've broken self-editing into four internal passes—content, organization, writing, and technical—plus an optional feedback pass.

Complete the four internal passes in order. After each one, you'll see a "stop here" page. Stop there, do that pass on your manuscript, then move to the next one. To clarify, a pass doesn't necessarily mean reading your entire manuscript. Each editing checklist will guide you to the specific sections or elements you need to review for that particular editing topic.

> If the idea of multiple passes overwhelms you, you have options:
>
> First, consider reading or skimming only what you need for your chosen topics—each editing checklist will guide you to the specific sections or elements you need to review. Alternatively, you could just do the content and writing pass to get the most bang for your buck, then hand it over to your editor without having done all the passes.
>
> Yes, completing all four passes will give you the best results. But I don't want to overwhelm you if this is your first foray into self-editing.

Then you have the feedback pass, which still belongs in the self-editing process but differs from the internal passes because it introduces outside perspectives, beta readers and critique partners.

You have two good options for when to do the feedback pass:

- After the content and organization passes: Do your big-picture revision first (content and organization), then get critique partner and/or beta reader feedback, and come back to the writing and technical passes afterward.
- After all four internal passes: Do organization, content, writing, and technical on your own, then get outside feedback on a more polished draft.

If you choose the first option, then jump to the feedback pass after the organization pass.

Don't go wild like I did! I had my beta readers giving me feedback at the same time I was self-editing this book. Long story about why it played out that way. But that meant my beta readers just ended up giving feedback on things I had already noticed and fixed.

EDITING TOPICS

Don't try to edit for every editing topic in a single pass. Instead, focus on *two or three* editing topics in each pass that you know are weak spots for you—either ones you've noticed or ones others have pointed out. For example, when doing your one or two content passes, you might choose to edit for create an effective introduction, unnecessary repetition, and reader-friendly content, not all six concepts.

To help with picking your editing priorities, I'm currently developing a manuscript diagnostic tool designed to work alongside this guide. The tool is intended to help you identify which editing topics are most important for your specific manuscript, along with a small number of example revisions in my editing style, so you can focus your revision time where it will matter most (see appendix A for more information).

SELF-EDITING IN PRACTICE

Each editing topic includes a practice section. Before you read my revision, try editing the example yourself. (I revised each example to address only that specific editing topic, leaving other potential issues unchanged.)

Note: The self-editing in practice sections come from various sources:

- My original examples
- AI-generated examples from ChatGPT or Claude (always noted)
- Anonymized examples from previous clients' manuscripts, used with permission

After the practice section, each topic includes a checklist you can use to revise your manuscript for that topic. You'll also find the master checklist in appendix C.

PERSONALIZED WORKBOOK

You can create a customized workbook for each pass that includes only the self-editing in practice exercises and editing steps for your chosen topics. This way, you can practice editing those passages in a Word document or print them out and edit by hand. Then use your customized checklist to apply the concepts to your manuscript.

At the start of each pass or "stop here" page, use the link or QR code to select your topics and generate a custom workbook for that pass.

A QUICK NOTE ABOUT REPETITION

Because you'll be choosing your own path through this guide—selecting different topics in each editing pass—you may see certain concepts appear in more than one topic. That overlap is intentional; many skills naturally connect. I never reteach anything in full, but I may repeat a definition or briefly re-explain a concept you've already read about.

1. Pick two or three topics in each pass.

2. Read those editing topics and do the editing in practice exercises (you practice first, then check my revision).

3. Use the editing steps checklists to then revise your manuscript for your chosen topics in one or two passes.

4. Move on to the next pass and repeat.

ADDITIONAL RESOURCES

If you're looking for resources on your entire journey, check both appendices. Appendix A contains resources I created to help you with your self-editing, and appendix B includes some of my favorite author communities, book marketing programs, audiobook narration resources, courses, and recommended reading—basically a toolbox to help you with your entire journey.

Now remember: Self-editing is the beginning, not the end. Once you complete the work in this book, you still need to work with a professional editor.

But I'm going to help you do it. I'm gifting you The Professional Editing Roadmap. This free six-part email course walks you through every step of what comes next, from understanding the levels of editing and budgeting for them, to finding the right editor and knowing what to expect when you work together, to understanding how to implement their feedback.

Get it free at http://beaconpointservices.org/get-free-resource/. Check out the Gift for You page after the conclusion for a qr code and more information.

CONTENT PASS

I panicked when I started my own self-editing. I drafted this manuscript, then didn't look at it for a few weeks. And when I did, my heart stopped. *Why did I think this book would be useful? Authors will hate it. I have nothing of substance here.*

Of course, this was just my imposter syndrome coming out to play. And I had some beta readers talk me off the edge. I know my content matters. Most likely yours does too. But just because the topic matters doesn't mean *your* book does. You have to have compelling and complete content.

And that's why this content pass matters—because you can focus on the *what* of your book, evaluating whether your ideas are compelling, your information is sufficient without being overwhelming, and your content delivers on what you've promised readers.

And then after you've done this content pass, if you still panic, tell your imposter syndrome to go stuff itself. Or just stuff yourself with lots of pie. Works every time.

Remember, don't try to tackle every topic at once. Instead, choose the two or three that match your biggest pain points and only look at what you need to for that topic.

I'm also developing a manuscript diagnostic tool designed to help authors pinpoint their highest-priority editing topics more quickly and accurately, using an editorial eye rather than an author's eye. If you'd like to learn more about this upcoming resource or sign up to get notified when it's ready, see appendix A. In the meantime, I offer a Manuscript Checkup service that provides personalized guidance to help you decide what to self-edit for (see appendix A).

But in general, if your manuscript struggles with . . .

Flat, dry content:

- Create an effective introduction (page 12)
- Strengthen chapter hooks (page 20)
- Ensure reader-friendly content (page 42)

Saying the same thing ten times:

- Delete unnecessary repetition (page 26)
- Ensure reader-friendly content (page 42)

Clarity of genre or beta readers say, "not what I expected":

- Align genre and audience expectations (page 52)
- Add necessary information (page 33)

Personalized workbook: To generate your customizable content pass workbook, scan the QR code or visit https://beaconpointservices.org/nonfiction-editing-workbook.

For best results, open on a computer or tablet to download and edit the Word document.

Create an Effective Introduction

I've got news for you: Many nonfiction authors have covered your topic (nothing new under the sun and all), which means your book must grab attention immediately. Your topic alone will not wow them unless you're explaining how to get kids to bed without a fight and keep them there all night long. I would read the heck out of that book. But typically, if your unique angle doesn't appear early, readers may think they've seen it all before and lose interest.

Don't begin your book with sweeping generalizations. To capture and keep the attention of your readers, use an engaging hook at the beginning of your book and at the start of every chapter.

You only get one chance to make a first impression. The introduction should show readers—quickly and clearly—why your book is worth their time. Trust me on this, I've edited many a dry introduction that just isn't going to get the reader turning the page.

Some *overexplain*, diving too deep into background information before engaging the reader. Don't do this. Your reader isn't as patient as a spouse who loves you. Others miss the *opportunity to connect,* making their introduction feel dry and academic rather than engaging and conversational.

When done well, an introduction pulls readers in and makes them feel like they're in the right place, both in topic and voice.

Elements of a strong introduction

HOOK

A good hook speaks directly to your reader by offering these elements:

- Thought-provoking question
- Powerful quote
- Interesting statistic
- Startling fact or bold statement
- Exciting anecdote
- Relatable scenario that speaks to the reader's pain points

Notice it says "thought-provoking question," not just question. My eighth-grade students loved to write hooks like "Have you ever heard of Michael Jordan?" or "Do you like to play Minecraft?" Yeah . . . those aren't hooks.

And don't think that just dropping a quote at the start of the chapter means you have a hook. If you have a profound quote, and then follow it up with boring drivel, your quote will not do you any good.

For some examples, check out the examples listed in "Strengthen Chapter Hooks" (page 21).

PROMISE VALUE

Show readers why the book should matter to them. Readers pick up a nonfiction book because they're looking for something: solutions, guidance, transformation, or even just clarity.

If you give them a strong promise, then they know they're in the right place and that they can trust you and your book to solve their problems. Without a clear promise, readers may lose interest before they even reach the first chapter.

To craft an effective promise, consider:

- Identifying the reader's core problem or goal
- Explaining how your book will help
- Setting expectations

Example:

> Many professionals are experts in their field but struggle to explain their ideas clearly in writing. So their strong insights get buried under jargon, cluttered sentences, or weak organization.
>
> This book will help you turn your expertise into clear, effective writing so readers can easily follow your ideas and enjoy reading your book. By the end, you'll have practical tools to turn rough drafts into polished, professional writing.

Avoid turning this promise into a long explanation. I often trim introductions that overload readers with details better saved for the chapter content. You can explain how your book will help without getting into the details.

PROVIDE CREDIBILITY

You aren't just selling your topic; you're selling you. I guarantee you, someone somewhere has written about your topic. The value you promise can most likely be found in hundreds of different books.

So why your book by you?

To sell your reader on you, share your experience and expertise with the topic. It should be a no-brainer that the reader needs to know what you know about the topic. But some forget to let their voice shine. Crack some jokes. Use unique words. Whatever is truly you.

Example:

> I've spent nine years editing nearly three hundred manuscripts, which means I've seen it all: brilliant ideas hidden under jargon and paragraphs that wander like they're sightseeing.
>
> Helping writers clean that up is an editor's job. But editors should be taking your book to the next level, not digging it out of a sentence-shaped avalanche. So I wrote this book based on the exact fixes I've made in hundreds of manuscripts.

GIVE A ROADMAP

Yes, give a roadmap, but for the love of everything holy, please don't list every topic, complete with definitions and examples, for every chapter and section.

Example of an unnecessary roadmap:

> In chapter 1, you'll learn how to create a clear vision for your business. Chapter 2 will dive into marketing strategies that drive results, while chapter 3 focuses on building a solid team. (Etc., etc.)

The reader can look at the table of contents to see that.

At least this example keeps the roadmap short. I've edited introductions where the roadmap turned into a full paragraph explaining every chapter.

This annoys many nonfiction readers. Get into the content as soon as possible. *Okay, but you said to create a roadmap.* Yes, yes, I did. But make this short and snappy.

To write an effective roadmap:

- Give readers a high-level overview of key concepts and strategies you will cover—essentially your overarching themes.
- Clarify the format or approach. For example, mention if they can expect to find case studies, action steps, stories, or practical tips. Let them know if you provide additional resources, worksheets, checklists, etc.
- Build anticipation without giving everything away. Leave them begging for you to get to the content, not because your introduction drags on but because they're excited.
- Reassure the reader they're ready and fully equipped to dive into the content. Encourage them to take their time, embrace the process, etc.

Self-editing in practice

Rewrite the introduction to include all the key elements.

Original introduction (for purposes of this guide, I made the intro short):

> Productivity is defined as the ability to produce something efficiently, to do the things that matter most without burning out. People have been writing about productivity for centuries, starting with early philosophers and continuing through the Industrial Revolution and into the modern age of technology.
>
> In this book, I want to talk about how you can be more productive in your daily life rather than letting your day slip away in a blur of emails, interruptions, and tasks. There are a lot of books out there on this topic, but I believe I have something valuable to offer because I've studied and worked with a lot of clients on this topic.

In chapter 1, we'll talk about setting goals. In chapter 2, we'll move on to time management techniques like batching, prioritization, and time blocking. Chapter 3 will cover tools and software you can use to track tasks, and chapter 4 will explore the science of habits and how to break bad ones. I'll also talk about how I've learned to be more productive in my own life over the years. I hope you find this book helpful.

> ## PAUSE HERE
>
> Open your personalized workbook on your computer and review the practice exercise, asking
>
> - Does this introduction grab your attention right away?
> - Can you clearly see the hook, the promise to the reader, the author's credibility, and a roadmap?
> - Where does it feel generic, flat, or overexplained before it connects?
>
> After answering, create a revised introduction before reading mine.

Problems with original:

It doesn't have a hook, the promise to the reader and the author's credibility are vague, and the roadmap is a chapter-by-chapter summary.

Revised introduction (I labeled each piece just for learning purposes):

[hook]

Ever end your day wondering where all the time went despite feeling busy from morning to night?

You're not alone, and you're definitely not broken. Many struggle with the gap between intention and execution. We know what we want to accomplish, but somehow our days slip away in a blur of emails, interruptions, and tasks that seemed urgent but weren't actually important.

[promise value]

This book will help you bridge that gap. Instead of adding more complexity to your already full plate, we're going to focus on clarity and sustainable systems that actually fit your life. You won't find rigid formulas here—just practical approaches that you can adapt to your unique situation and goals.

[roadmap]

Throughout this book, you'll discover frameworks for identifying your true priorities, practical techniques for managing your time and energy, and tools for building habits that support your goals rather than overwhelming you. Each chapter includes actionable strategies you can implement immediately, along with real examples and the flexibility to customize approaches based on what works best for you.

Along the way, I'll challenge some common advice, help you experiment with what fits, and encourage you to make this process your own. Whether you read it cover to cover or bounce around to what speaks loudest to you, you'll come away with clarity, confidence, a sustainable system, and a productivity rhythm that supports your real goals, *not just your never-ending to-do list.*

[credibility]

I've spent years studying productivity methods, testing them in my own life, and working with clients who needed real solutions. And the main thing I've learned is that productivity is about doing what matters most, efficiently and without burning out. Through trial and error (plenty of error), I've discovered what actually works for busy people with real constraints and responsibilities.

[promise value]

By the time you finish this book, you'll have a flexible, personalized system to get stuff done *without* burning out or becoming someone you don't even recognize.

So, if you're tired of spinning your wheels and want a productivity approach that feels human, doable, and maybe even *fun*, you're in the right place. Let's do this.

Your intro can be longer than this, especially the credibility section. But for purposes of this guide, I need to keep examples relatively short.

EDITING STEPS

- ❑ Mark each key element in your introduction (hook, promise value, provide credibility, roadmap) and add in any you're missing.
- ❑ Revise if your chapter overview contains a chapter-by-chapter, topic-by-topic breakdown.
- ❑ Add in your voice and personality where applicable.
- ❑ Delete any content that veers into overexplaining territory.

Strengthen Chapter Hooks

If your chapter beginnings don't grip the reader, why should your reader trust the rest? It sucks, but it's true. Social media hooks are the death of me. I can't capture attention that quickly. Luckily, you have a little longer with a book. But you still gotta capture and keep that attention.

A good hook speaks directly to your reader by offering these elements:

- Thought-provoking question
- Powerful quote
- Interesting statistic
- Startling fact or bold statement
- Exciting anecdote
- Relatable scenario that speaks to the reader's pain points

Notice it says "thought-provoking question," not just question. My eighth-grade students loved to write hooks like "Have you ever heard of Michael Jordan?" or "Do you like to play Minecraft?" Yeah . . . those aren't hooks.

And don't think that just dropping a quote at the start of the chapter means you have a hook. If you have a profound quote and then follow it up with boring drivel, your quote will not do you any good.

> **Epigraphs**
>
> This is different from inserting a quote at the start of every chapter separated from your content. Those are called epigraphs and aren't your hook.

Examples of effective hooks

THOUGHT-PROVOKING QUESTION AND QUOTE COMBINATION

> Brad Montague said, "Dreamers are many, but doers are few." What separates the dreamers from the doers? How can you actively become a doer? You have been told all your life: create a goal, act on it, then create another goal, and act on it, etc. This constant path of creating and then acting will mold you into the person you want to become, bringing lasting happiness.

ANECDOTE

An anecdote can be an experience/story from your own life or that of others. Either way, it serves as an effective hook because people love stories. They love learning from the lives of others.

This anecdote example comes from *A 2nd Helping of Chicken Soup for the Soul*.[1] For purposes of keeping this short, I have summarized the story. But do note, you can have a longer anecdote as your hook. Not so long that readers get impatient, but longer than what I have here.

---

1 Jack Canfield and Mark Victor Hansen, *A 2nd Helping of Chicken Soup for the Soul: 101 More Stories to Open the Heart and Rekindle the Spirit* (Deerfield Beach, FL: Health Communications, 1995).

Major James Nesmeth completely quit golf for seven years. He never touched a club or stepped onto a course. The first time he returned, he shot a 74—despite not having practiced once.

The first step to achieving your goal is to visualize.

QUOTE

Steven Spielberg said, "Technology can be our best friend, and technology can also be the biggest party pooper of our lives. It interrupts our own story, interrupts our ability to have a thought or a daydream, to imagine something wonderful because we're too busy bridging the walk from the cafeteria back to the office on the cell phone."[2] As Steven noted, cell phones can negatively affect adults who have not had the time to mature and develop their story, so imagine how much this affects the life of a young teenager.

QUESTIONS

- "While cell phones are becoming a given in teenagers' lives, are they doing more harm than good?"
- "What would you do if you could play God for a day? That's exactly what the leaders of the tiny island nation of Guam tried to answer."[3]

---

2   "Spielberg in the Twilight Zone," Wired, June 1, 2002, https://www.wired.com/2002/06/spielberg/.

3   "Essay Hooks Ideas," University of Wisconsin-Madison Psychology 225, accessed October 22, 2025, https://online225.psych.wisc.edu/wp-content/uploads/225-Master/225-UnitPages/Unit-03/PSY-225_Gernsbacher_Hooks.pdf.

BOLD STATEMENT

Everything you've been taught about productivity is wrong. Hustle culture glorifies long hours, multitasking, and never taking breaks, but science shows these habits sabotage your success. If you're tired of spinning your wheels and feeling exhausted, you need to rethink how you approach your work and life. This book will show you a better way.

Self-editing in practice

Identify why the original hook is weak and strengthen it.

Original A:

"Do you know how to achieve your goals? If you don't, I will walk you through the five most important steps to achieving your goals."

PAUSE HERE

Open your personalized workbook on your computer and review the practice exercise, asking

- Does this opening truly hook you, or does it feel obvious or generic?

- What type of hook (question, story, bold statement, quote, statistic) is it trying to be, and is it compelling enough?

- Where could the author use a more vivid, specific, or surprising angle?

After answering, create a new hook before viewing mine.

Problem with original A:

Yes, it begins with a question, one of the hook types, but it's not a thought-provoking question. It's a simple yes or no. Plus, so many books talk about how to create goals.

Revised A (two ideas):

- Ninety-two percent of people never achieve their New Year's resolutions, not because they're lazy but because they skip the one thing that matters most. (startling fact)
- What if the reason you're not reaching your goals isn't a lack of motivation but a lack of strategy?

Original B:

Communication is important in relationships. Without good communication, misunderstandings happen and conflicts arise. In this chapter, we'll discuss how to communicate better with your partner so you can have a healthier relationship.

PAUSE HERE

- Does this opening truly hook you, or does it feel obvious or generic?
- What type of hook (question, story, bold statement, quote, statistic) is it trying to be, and is it compelling enough?
- Where could the author use a more vivid, specific, or surprising angle?

After answering, create a new hook before you read my revision.

Problem with original B:

This opening is bland and states the obvious. It reads like a thesis statement from a high school essay, and it lacks a real hook.

Revised B (three ideas):

- "You're not listening!" she yelled, tears streaming down her face. He was listening, or so he thought. But somewhere between his ears and his understanding, her words got lost. This scene plays out in relationships every day because people have never learned how to truly hear each other. (relatable scenario/anecdote)
- The number one predictor of divorce is poor communication. Yet most of us were never taught how to do it well. (startling fact)
- What if the biggest communication problem in your relationship isn't what you say, but what you assume the other person already knows? (thought-provoking question)

EDITING STEPS

- ❑ Pause at the end of the first paragraph or first few paragraphs of every chapter and ask if you have an engaging hook. If not, revise.
- ❑ Identify the hook types you use and make sure not to use the same type in every chapter.

Delete Unnecessary Repetition

Repeat after me: I will not pull a Katie. Pulling a "Katie" means explaining things three times in three different ways. I have this annoying habit (just ask my poor husband), stemming from my miscommunication anxiety trigger. But, man, do I spend a lot of time deleting repetitive content in clients' manuscripts. It's harder to do in our own writing. We believe we need all. the. words.

But you don't, not if you're just saying the same thing over and over. So pay attention to repetitive information.

Most readers get impatient when they read something twice. And if they don't feel impatient, they may feel insulted. *I got it the first time around, buddy!*

This doesn't mean you can't have any repetition. Repetition can help with learning. But overdoing it can frustrate readers and make your content feel redundant. The key is intentional repetition for learning purposes versus unintentional repetition, or overexplaining because you're worried they won't get it.

Trust that your reader paid attention, understood it, and still remembers the information several chapters later. Now, this doesn't mean you can't summarize key points in a dense chapter. But if the chapter isn't long or complex, even a summary of key points can feel redundant.

Typical problematic spots to pay attention to

As you revise, watch for areas where redundancies often sneak in.

CHAPTER SUMMARIES

Chapter summaries naturally repeat information, but you can still keep them fresh by focusing on key takeaways instead of rehashing every point. If the chapter was fairly straightforward and focused on one or two main topics without any subtopics, then you probably don't even need a chapter summary.

If the chapter had a lot of subtopics, then you may want to provide a review. But consider creating a bulleted list of key insights, reflection questions, or action steps to reframe the idea with new language or provide examples so the content stays fresh and engaging rather than a full-on summary.

EXPLAINING COMPLEX CONCEPTS

First, trust that your reader will get it even if that feels difficult. Trust me! I struggle with this too, often explaining a concept at least three times, in three different ways, to make sure people understand me. Miscommunication triggers my anxiety, so I overcompensate. But doing so annoys people, and it annoys me.

(Did you notice the repetition here? This is an example of unnecessary repetition. I used the same hook in this section that I did in the introduction for the chapter. Usually, authors don't do this just mere paragraphs later, but over the course of their whole book, they end up using the same hook or anecdote in multiple places.)

When explaining a complex topic, you want to ensure your readers understand, but if you're just saying the same thing in different words, then that's unnecessary repetition.

Original:

> Compounding interest means you earn interest not just on your original money, but on the interest you've already earned. In other words, your interest earns interest. So it's like a snowball rolling downhill: The snow that's already attached picks up more snow, making the ball bigger, which then picks up even more snow. And the longer you wait, the faster it grows. It's a cycle where each gain feeds the next gain (generated by Claude).

A metaphor can certainly help a reader understand a complex concept when the explanation alone doesn't quite suffice. But here the concept was clear before the unnecessary metaphor.

Revised:

> Compounding interest is like a snowball rolling downhill, as you earn interest on your interest, not just your original money. The longer you wait, the faster it grows.

Still used the metaphor to help them understand the concept but without repeating the explanation.

While overexplaining is a problem, sometimes even one explanation is repetitive if it states something the audience already knows. So try to think like your reader and determine what your target audience already knows and what they need to know. If you have a wide target audience and some will not understand the basics and others will, then you will need to explain concepts some readers already know. But be mindful of this and keep the basic part short and sweet.

Original:

> The stock market is where people buy and sell shares of companies. Investors purchase stock in companies they hope will grow, causing the value of their shares to increase. Because the market fluctuates, investors try to make decisions that will help them earn more money over time.
>
> One strategy investors use is dollar-cost averaging.

Most people already understand the general idea of the stock market, so the background explanation isn't necessary. The focus should be on the concept the reader actually needs to learn.

Revised:

> One strategy investors use is dollar-cost averaging: investing a fixed amount of money at regular intervals regardless of market price.

Tip

Ask someone in your target audience whether you've over-explained concept X. The feedback only helps if it comes from the right readers.

For example, my husband works as an electrical engineer, and science was the only subject in school I didn't understand. He could never overexplain to me because I need all the explanations. So it wouldn't do him any good to ask me.

REFERENCING AN EARLIER-MENTIONED IDEA

When you revisit a previously mentioned idea to build on it, use cues such as "as we explored earlier" or "to build on our previous discussion" to guide the reader forward. Your goal is to add something new, though, not just reference it. So give a fresh insight or example.

Example:

> As we discussed earlier, consistency is key in building habits. A recent study by [researcher's name] further emphasizes this by showing how daily practice increases skill retention by 50 percent.

REINFORCING AN IMPORTANT POINT

Sometimes you want to repeat something for emphasis. After all, we learn through repetition. In that case, reframe the idea with new language or examples so the content stays fresh and engaging and doesn't feel like a copy-paste job. For example, in this book, I remind readers to just pick two or three topics in each pass, but I don't say it the exact same way every time. The repetition, though, is important to help my readers avoid overwhelm.

Self-editing in practice

Spot the repetition in the original and decide whether it's the good kind or not. If not, revise it accordingly.

Original:

> Time management is crucial for anyone trying to run a successful business. If you want your business to thrive, managing your time effectively is non-negotiable. Poor time management can lead to

missed deadlines, burnout, and frustration. When you don't have a good handle on your schedule, it's easy to fall behind. And once you're behind, it's harder to get back on track.

That's why learning how to manage your time well is one of the most important skills for business owners. Time management affects everything from your ability to meet client expectations to your own mental well-being. If you're constantly putting out fires, you'll never have time to grow your business intentionally (generated by ChatGPT).

PAUSE HERE

Open your personalized workbook on your computer and review the practice exercise, asking

- Which ideas or phrases feel repetitive and don't add anything new?

- If you had to boil this down to the essential message, what would you keep and what would you cut or combine?

- Where could one stronger sentence replace several weaker, repetitive ones?

After answering, revise the passage before checking what I did.

Problem with original:

The core message (time management is important) is stated multiple times with different phrasing, with many of the examples having overlap in meaning.

Revised:

> Time management is crucial for anyone trying to run a success-ful business.
>
> When you don't have a good handle on your schedule, it's easy to fall behind. This can lead to burnout and poor client relationships, ultimately affecting your well-being. And once you're at this point, it's harder to get back on track.

I deleted the original second and third sentences. The second was completely redundant, and the third only had one new idea that I just moved to later. I deleted the redundant information found in the second paragraph and integrated what was new from the first into the second.

EDITING STEPS

- ❑ Highlight phrases, concepts, or anecdotes that appear frequently.
- ❑ Look at what you have highlighted and delete any redundant and unnecessary content, rephrase any necessary content for reinforcement, or merge it with earlier content discussing the same concept.

Add Necessary Information

In the last topic, we deleted unnecessary information. Now we're adding necessary information. Yes, editing is apparently brought to you by the same logic as giving extra credit right after taking points off a quiz.

But how do you know what and where to add? This one can be tricky. You may think you've fully explained your idea because *you* understand it. When **you** wrote the sentence, you also supplied the context, assumptions, and background information mentally, even if none of that made it onto the page.

So, to know where you have gaps and need more information to ensure the reader doesn't feel confused, use the strategies below.

Notice your "leaps"

Writers often jump from point A to point C because the connection feels obvious to them, but readers need point B.

Ask:

- Did I move too quickly from setup to conclusion?
- Did I claim something without explaining why it's true?
- Did I introduce a new concept and then immediately shift topics?

Clue you may need more info: Two sentences feel like they go together only because you know what you meant, but the reasoning isn't spelled out on the page.

Original:

> Nonfiction books often fail because of weak introductions. That's why you should start your book with a promise to the reader.
>
> *This jumps from the problem to the solution without explaining how it's the solution.*

Revised:

> Nonfiction books often fail because of weak introductions. If readers can't quickly see why the book matters to them, they may lose interest before reaching the first chapter. So start your book with a clear promise to the reader.

Another type of leap is using words you know, but the reader might not know.

Ask:

- Have I used a term that someone new to this field might not be familiar with?
- Have I introduced an acronym without defining it?
- Would someone outside my circle understand what this word or phrase means?

If you're writing to beginners, err on the side of defining terms.

If you're writing to experienced readers, err on the side of brevity but clarity.

Identify where you've described what, but not how

This is a common gap. You've told them what to do, but not how. And this can frustrate readers.

Examples:

> "Set healthy boundaries."

Okay, but how?

> "Improve your website messaging."

Great. But what does that look like?

When you give an instruction, ask:

- Did I teach them how to do this?
- Did I offer examples, templates, or phrasing my readers can copy?
- Did I give at least one concrete scenario?

If any section feels inspirational but not actionable, you should add more information.

Ask "but why" like a kid

Okay, don't go to extremes with this like my kids, but sometimes wisdom comes from asking "but why?"

Examples:

> Research shows habit stacking works. → But why does that work?
> This tool changed my workflow. → But why? What changed?
> Consistency is key. → But why is it important?

If you anticipate the reader's questions and answer them, the content feels complete.

Deliver on your promise

Each chapter and section in your book makes a promise to your reader. You must deliver it. This promise may come from the title, section heading, opening paragraph, etc. It may not be explicit, but every book has a promise.

Example (promise for this chapter):

> But how do you know what and when to add? This one can be tricky. You may think you've fully explained your idea because *you* understand it. When you wrote the sentence, you also supplied the context, assumptions, and background information mentally, even if none of that made it onto the page.

> *If I hadn't given specific how-tos in this chapter, then I wouldn't have delivered on the promise. Ironically, my first draft didn't have how-tos. I had explained the importance of this topic but didn't have examples explaining how to do it. I read the lesson and was like, "Whoops, I need to add a whole lot more content to the 'add necessary information' topic."*

If your chapter doesn't fulfill the promise, add information or change the promise.

When in doubt, add one more item

If you're unsure whether the information is sufficient for a beginner, add one more

- definition
- scenario
- example
- practical step
- tip
- or clarifying sentence

One more won't cause your readers to think, "Okay, I get it," (unless the concept has already been made very clear, but in that case, you wouldn't have flagged it as potentially needing more information), but it could help your reader better understand.

Self-editing in practice

Original A:

> Many people struggle with setting boundaries because they were never taught how to express their needs. When you lack models for healthy communication, it's easy to fall into people-pleasing or overcommitting. Learning to say no is an essential part of personal growth, and it often requires unlearning old habits.
>
> Boundaries aren't about being selfish—they're about being clear. When you communicate honestly, you give others the opportunity to do the same. While setting boundaries may feel uncomfortable at first, it becomes easier with practice. Over time, you'll find that your relationships become more balanced and respectful (generated by ChatGPT).

> ## PAUSE HERE
>
> Open your personalized workbook on your computer and review the practice exercise, asking
>
> - What feels vague, theoretical, or surface-level in this passage?
> - If a reader were brand new to this topic, what would they still be confused about?
>
> After answering, read my explanation of the issue, then revise the passage before checking mine.

Problems with original A:

This passage stays on the surface and remains mostly theoretical, offering broad encouragement without practical help. Without a clear definition of what a boundary is, a step-by-step example of how to set one, and real-life context to help the reader see themselves in the situation, they can't apply it.

Revised A:

After the first paragraph, you could add these two paragraphs:

> At its core, a boundary is simply a clear statement of what you will or won't accept. For example, a boundary might sound like, "I'm not available for work calls after 6 p.m." or "I'm happy to help with the event, but I can only contribute two hours." These statements are respectful but firm, and they help others know what to expect from you.
>
> If you're new to boundary-setting, start small. Think of one area in your life where you feel stretched too thin. What's one specific situation where you often say yes when you want to say no? Draft a short, polite response you can use next time. You might

even practice saying it out loud or writing it in an email to boost your confidence.

Original B:

> To grow your email list, you'll need a strong lead magnet. Once you have your lead magnet, connect it to your email service provider with an opt-in form and make sure your landing page is optimized for conversions. A/B test different headlines to see what gets the most engagement, and don't forget to nurture new subscribers with a welcome sequence (generated by ChatGPT).

PAUSE HERE

- Which terms or concepts might confuse a beginner?
- What key steps are mentioned but not fully explained?

After answering, add in some necessary information before seeing mine.

Potential problem with original B:

Depending on the target audience, this passage may need added details. If the target reader is new to email marketing, they might feel overwhelmed and frustrated with the undefined jargon. If they aren't, then this is fine as is.

Revised B:

> To grow your email list, start by creating a lead magnet, which is a free resource (like a checklist, guide, or template) that your target audience finds valuable enough to give you their email address in exchange for the freebie.

Once you have your lead magnet, use an email service provider like MailerLite, ConvertKit, or Mailchimp to manage your list. These platforms let you build opt-in forms—simple boxes where people enter their email to get your freebie. You'll also need a standalone web page that explains the value of your lead magnet and encourages people to sign up, known as the landing page. A good conversion rate means a high percentage of visitors are signing up.

Once your setup is live, monitor how it performs. To do this, test different headlines to see what gets the most engagement, known as A/B testing. Finally, once someone joins your list, welcome them with an automated welcome sequence, a series of two to five emails that introduce you, deliver the freebie, and offer a few helpful tips to build trust.

I added more details to explain the jargon.

EDITING STEPS

❑ Pause anytime you're describing a new concept and ask these questions. If you answer no to the first two or yes to the others, add in the necessary details.

- Have you defined it clearly and given strong, concrete examples, answering all the "but whys" that your reader needs to know?
- Have you assumed prior knowledge that your reader may not have?
- Have you explained how content relates to each other rather than leaping from one to the other?
- Do you have any terms, acronyms, or industry jargon that your target reader may stumble over?
- Could a visual aid (table, checklist, step-by-step summary) help clarify your point?

❑ Pause anytime you have a personal story and ask if this story is balanced with actionable takeaways? (You want to include your own experiences—just ensure they serve the reader, not your ego.) If not, make sure to include the takeaway from the story unless it's implied. You don't want to insult the reader by stating the obvious.

❑ At the end of each chapter, ask these questions. If the answer is no, add in the necessary details.

- Did you deliver on the promise of the chapter?
- Does this chapter offer practical insights (a clear how) and original thinking, not just theory or surface-level advice (unless you intended for this chapter to be theoretical, but you shouldn't have too many of those)?

Ensure Reader-Friendly Content

Some nonfiction books are quite boring and not reader friendly. Jordan Ring, author of *Nonfiction Alchemy*, called this a "big, slimy, megalodon-level problem."[4] While he meant more than just boredom and was also calling out mindless drivel, we already fixed that in a previous topic: deleting unnecessary content. But boredom remains a factor. If your reader falls asleep on their cat (hey, don't judge . . . fur is softer than a desk) while reading your book, you've got a problem.

Let's explore what actually keeps readers engaged since they're the ones who ultimately decide whether a book succeeds.

Reader-friendly strategies

SHARE STORIES

Don't run wild and turn your nonfiction book into a memoir (unless it is one), but do include stories—your own, others' stories, or ones you've learned from. You don't need to turn these into full scenes with dialogue, narrative beats, and dramatic action. But you need stories. Why? Because our brains love stories. They stick with us in ways that dry facts don't. (If you're curious to know the science behind this, check out the book, *The*

---

4   Jordan Ring, *Nonfiction Alchemy (self-published, 2024).*

Science of Storytelling: Why Stories Make Us Human and How to Tell Them Better.[5])

- Writing a medical how-to or self-help book? Share successful and unsuccessful case studies.
- Writing a how-to guide? Share yours and others' successes and failures.
- Writing a religious guidebook? Share how people's lives changed for the better.

Example:

> You can reduce your HbA1c levels through a change in diet and regular exercise, like Tom.
>
> At 54, Tom was injecting insulin twice a day. His doctor suggested one change: Cut the carbs and walk thirty minutes after dinner. Three months later, Tom's A1C had dropped enough to stop the injections entirely.

Adding in that quick success story gives your statement credibility and keeps the reader more engaged.

You can also use made-up stories. Just don't present a made-up story as fact (e.g., implying it was one of your clients).

Use made-up stories like

- blending multiple real people's stories into one
- using the reader as the character (You've just gotten the diagnosis. Your hands are shaking . . .)
- sharing a day in the life (walking through a made-up person's typical day)

---

5   Will Storr, *The Science of Storytelling: Why Stories Make Us Human and How to Tell Them Better* (New York: Abrams Press, 2020).

- inserting a cautionary tale (a made-up person who does everything wrong so you can show what not to do)
- including made-up dialogue snippets (fictional conversation that shows a dynamic or problem)

Original:

> Failing to set boundaries with clients early in a business relationship often leads to scope creep, resentment, and burnout.

Revised:

> Imagine a freelancer, Linda, landed her first big client, and she said yes to every last-minute request. A quick logo tweak. One more revision. Eight months later she is working weekends, charging her original rate, and dreading their name in her inbox. Set boundaries early, or your clients will set them for you.

> *I inserted a made-up cautionary tale to prove the point. Notice I didn't say, "When Linda landed . . . " which sounds like the story is based on a real client.*

Original:

> Caregivers who don't schedule time for themselves often experience gradual emotional exhaustion that goes unnoticed until it becomes a crisis.

Revised:

> A typical day for a caregiver often looks like this: By 7 a.m. Carol had given her mother breakfast, sorted her medications, and fielded a call from the home health agency. By noon she'd canceled

her own doctor's appointment—again. She told herself she'd rest on Sunday. The same thing she'd been saying for four months. *If you don't put yourself on the schedule, you won't make it.*

If you struggle with this, follow Jonathan Jordan on LinkedIn and check out his book, *Start with Story: How Great Storytellers Transform Ideas into Impact.* He helps people find their inner storyteller and turns everything into story, blending insights from both fiction and nonfiction.

Now, you don't want to overshoot this and give too much story. Each anecdote shouldn't exceed two hundred words unless it's central to your argument. And you'll always want to end with what it shows and why it matters to the reader; otherwise, it just sounds like you're adding in story for story's sake.

DON'T BE TOO ACADEMIC

If you're writing for the general public, avoid jargon and toss out essay-writing advice you learned in school. As a former English teacher, I can tell you that much of what I taught is still valuable—many of those lessons apply directly to writing a book. But forget the essay paragraph structure. That structure helps with convincing or informing in a short format, not for a book. Books need to maintain interest for a hundred or more pages. A predictable essay structure becomes monotonous and can make your reader feel like they're being lectured to.

So don't begin your chapters with a thesis statement, or worse, "This chapter is about [insert quick overview of every subtopic in the chapter]." And don't end each chapter with a conclusion that restates the thesis "Now that you've learned about XYZ . . . " Look, you can start with an overview of sorts and end with a summary, but if it sounds like an essay, then just no. This takes readers back to their school days, and many students say, "English class is boring." (Except, of course, not my students. After all, I tap danced and rapped for them.)

Original chapter opening:

> A "small revision" becomes a full rewrite. A client expects instant replies at all hours. Sound familiar? This chapter explains why boundaries matter, how to communicate them effectively, and how maintaining them can lead to greater long-term success.

Revised chapter opening:

> A "small revision" becomes a full rewrite. A client expects instant replies at all hours. Sound familiar? This doesn't usually happen because a person is intentionally trying to take advantage of you. It happens because boundaries were never clearly set in the first place. Understanding where your limits are—and how to communicate them—can change the entire way you work with clients.

Notice they have the same hook, which is fine. Hook writing applies to essays and books, but the revised works better for a book as it implies the topic instead of formally announcing it, and it signals the direction of the chapter without sounding like an essay outline.

The same goes for jargon. If you're a doctor, pastor, lawyer, CEO, or [insert job title here], don't write as if your readers are your colleagues. Unless, of course, your colleagues are your audience. Every industry has specialized terms, and that's fine. Just explain them clearly when you need to use them.

Original:

> We implemented a multi-modal therapeutic intervention to improve patient outcomes.
>
> *Readers don't need to know the term "multi-modal therapeutic intervention." This is unnecessary jargon that serves no purpose.*

Revised:

> We used several treatment approaches to help patients improve.

Original:

> You'll want to monitor your conversion rate.
>
> *The reader will encounter the jargon "conversation rate" on their analytics dashboard, so it's necessary jargon, but depending on your audience, you may need to define it.*

Revised:

> You'll want to monitor your conversion rate, which is the percentage of people who take the action you want—such as signing up for your email list or buying your product.

I've edited medical self-help books written like peer-reviewed journal articles. I had to reread sections while stress-eating sugar. Your readers don't want to work that hard.

Plain language editors exist for a reason: Nobody wants to slog through a dry, technical book. They already had to do that in school.

INCLUDE THE READER

To include the reader, write directly to them using "you" and "we." Reserve "I" for personal stories. When teaching or offering action steps, choose "you" over "we"—it's more powerful and direct.

Original:

> When I work with business owners, I always start by mapping out the customer journey. I analyze where prospects first encounter the brand and where they drop off. Once I understand that process, I redesign the funnel to improve conversions.
>
> *This is a whole lot of "I." And it's not a personal story. This is just explaining what the author does, but ultimately, they want the reader to do this.*

Revised:

> When you map out your customer journey, start by identifying where prospects first encounter your brand and where they may drop off. Once you understand that process, you can redesign the funnel to improve conversions.
>
> *"You" is better than "we" here because it's directing the reader to apply a concept.*

You can use "we" or "you" when discussing a collective experience, depending on your goals and the tone you're going for.

Example:

> When we launch a new product, we assume customers will see its value. After all, we sat with the idea for months and understand the problem it solves. But our customers are encountering it for the first time.

> **Tip**
>
> In your manuscript, search for "you" and see how many instances you have. Then search "I" and see how many instances you have.

Another way to include the reader is to provide something for them to do, such as action steps or reflection questions that prompt them to write down their answers. Don't just pose the question; give the reader space to answer it. Even if they can't write in an ebook, providing the space lets the reader know you're serious about wanting them to actually write an answer down.

Self-editing in practice

Imagine the original text comes from a general nonfiction book with a general audience, and think about how you could make it more reader friendly.

Original:

> Since the neurological mechanisms underlying automaticity involve synaptic strengthening in the basal ganglia, which facilitates procedural memory consolidation, habit formation requires the establishment of consistent behavioral patterns through systematic implementation of structured routines. Research indicates that individuals who utilize environmental cue-response frameworks demonstrate enhanced behavioral adherence rates compared to those employing unstructured approaches (generated by ChatGPT).

> ## PAUSE HERE
>
> Open your personalized workbook on your computer and review the practice exercise, asking
>
> - How does this passage feel to you as a reader—engaging or exhausting?
> - Where does jargon, density, or academic tone make the message harder to follow?
>
> After answering, revise the passage before reading mine.

Problems with original:

While this gets the point across, the tone is dry, the language is dense, and the reader is completely absent. It doesn't contain any stories, use "you" or "we," or offer practical application, just academic theory. Essentially, it's boring.

Revised:

> I used to leave my computer on with all my programs and internet tabs still open every day after work. This caused issues for my computer, but it was an ingrained habit. To course correct, I programmed my Alexa to remind me every day around 5 p.m. to close out of my programs and tabs and sleep my computer. I found a solution that worked: an extension called Session Buddy that stores my daily tabs and opens them when I request it. Now that Alexa reminds me and I've done it the same way every day, I don't even need the reminder anymore.
>
> This works because consistent repetition strengthens your brain connections, turning new behaviors into a habit. To form a new habit, establish a clear cue (like my Alexa reminder), make the

routine easy to follow (Session Buddy made closing tabs less annoying), and stick with it until it becomes second nature.

This revision removes the academic jargon ("systematic implementation" → clear cues, etc.), replaces abstract theory with a personal story, and shifts to direct "you" language.

EDITING STEPS

❏ If you don't have any stories (yours, others', or made-up ones), add some in. Make sure to connect them back to the reader so they serve a point.

❏ Define any necessary jargon.

❏ Rewrite any sentence or section that is reminiscent of an English essay.

❏ If you use "I" too often, rewrite to use more "you" and "we."

❏ Switch from "we" to "you" when giving action steps or lessons.

❏ Provide exercises, action steps, and/or questions for them to answer if it makes sense for your book.

Align Genre and Audience Expectations

How do you feel when you order something that sounds amazing, but then doesn't taste great? I once ordered a baklava shake. I love baklava. I love shakes. I do not love baklava shakes. In this case, the name got me, but sometimes the menu description sounds amazing—but the actual item disappoints.

Readers experience that same feeling when a book doesn't match their expectations. They pick up a book with certain genre and topic assumptions, and if those expectations aren't met, they may feel disappointed, no matter how strong the writing and content are. This can mean negative reviews.

So consider your genre and audience carefully. Genre is the promise you make, and your audience determines who that promise is for.

Common genre expectations

Since genre is the promise, I've included each genre's core promise.[6]

SELF-HELP

Promise: Help the reader solve a personal problem or meaningfully improve their life

---

6 AI initially drafted this subsection, then I edited the output.

Common expectations:

- Address a clear problem or challenge (e.g., anxiety, productivity, confidence)
- Provide actionable tips, strategies, or steps your reader can use
- Use an encouraging, empowering tone that builds trust
- Give personal anecdotes or case studies to illustrate points
- Ensure your chapters are digestible with a clear focus or theme
- Use some repetition for reinforcement (but not overkill)
- Add reflection questions, exercises, or journaling prompts

HOW-TO

Promise: Teach them how to do something specific, step by step

Common expectations:

- Include a step-by-step structure or logical sequence of tasks
- Give clear instructions without jargon
- Provide visual aids or examples (e.g., screenshots, checklists, diagrams, recipes)
- Reduce the fluff, get to the point quickly
- Troubleshoot tips or common mistakes to avoid
- Maintain a practical tone with a "teacher" or "coach" voice
- Optional: provide downloadable resources or companion tools

BUSINESS

Promise: Improve career, leadership, strategy, or entrepreneurial success

Common expectations:

- Prove your credibility (your background or expertise in the field)
- Provide case studies, research, or frameworks to back up claims
- Give clear takeaways or applications to real business scenarios

- Provide insight into trends, systems, or thought leadership
- Include charts, diagrams, or models
- Maintain a balanced tone: professional but not stiff
- Has a specific audience with a message tailored to them: executives, entrepreneurs, freelancers, etc.

RELIGIOUS OR SPIRITUAL GUIDEBOOKS

Promise: Deepen their faith, find spiritual guidance, or apply religious principles to life

Common expectations:

- Provide a blend of inspiration, teaching, and practical application
- Use Scripture references or quotes from sacred texts
- Use testimonies, parables, or stories of transformation
- Give reflection prompts, prayer suggestions, or journaling space
- Maintain a gentle, pastoral tone, encouraging, wise, not preachy
- Have a clear theological stance (denomination, worldview) and consistency
- Provide moral or spiritual takeaways tied to everyday life

Audience expectations

Clearly define your audience. If your audience is too generic (like "everyone" or "all women"), you can't serve them as well. The more specific you are, the more likely the message will truly serve them. This doesn't mean readers outside your target audience won't pick up your book; it simply ensures your ideal readers will find the book more reader friendly and engaging.

When you know your specific audience, you can avoid including what they already know, decide when to define or use jargon, and focus on explaining what they actually need.

Self-editing in practice

All included content should be on genre. So while the book as a whole might meet the genre expectations, the passages below need revision because they drift away from the tone and genre expectations. As you read the original, identify what doesn't align and then revise it.

Original A (Self-help book):

> This chapter will cover three major points about time management: the psychological roots of procrastination, the evolution of productivity systems in the twentieth century, and how attention spans have changed due to digital media.
>
> Historically, the development of timekeeping mechanisms in the eighteenth and nineteenth centuries directly influenced how people structured their work. Modern productivity owes a debt to Frederick Winslow Taylor's scientific management theory, which emphasized efficiency above all else. These frameworks persist today, though they've been modified for knowledge workers.
>
> The theoretical constructs discussed herein will be helpful for readers wishing to conceptualize the nature of modern time usage (generated by ChatGPT).

PAUSE HERE

Open your personalized workbook on your computer and review the practice exercise, asking

- If you picked this up as a self-help book, would this passage feel like the kind of tone and guidance you expect?

- Does it speak directly to the reader's problem and offer hope or help?

After answering, look at my explanation of the issues, then revise the passage before checking what I did.

Problems with original A:

Even if the book as a whole provides actionable steps and solves a problem, this passage isn't aligned with genre expectations. It reads like an academic research paper, not a self-help book, and it lacks an encouraging tone.

Revised A:

> If you're feeling overwhelmed by your to-do list and unsure where all your time goes, you're not alone. Most people never learned how to manage their time; they just react to what's urgent.
>
> Of course, procrastination happens, and it's not just laziness. To combat that, you need a schedule that fits your actual brain, protects your time from digital distractions, and allows you to choose what to keep and what to leave behind without feeling like a slave to the "productivity push."
>
> As you build your own time management system, it helps to understand where these ideas came from. We're all so obsessed with "productivity," which we inherited from the industrial age, when clocks started running the show and people were trained to work efficiently like machines.
>
> In fact, a guy named Frederick Winslow Taylor helped popularize the idea that every second counts and that you needed to optimize tasks to find success. And while his approach was designed for factory work, that mindset still shows up in how we treat our to-do lists today.
>
> But you're not a machine. And you don't need to pack your day full to the brim to be productive. You get to decide what productivity looks like for you.
>
> *I retained the historical facts, but clarified why they matter to the reader: they can release outdated productivity ideas. If the historical lesson didn't*

directly help the reader solve their problem, then it wouldn't belong at all, regardless of tone.

Original B (Business):

> I've been thinking lately about what it really means to fail. Not the clinical, post-mortem kind of failure analysis you do in a boardroom, but the 2 a.m. kind, when you're lying awake replaying a decision you can't undo. That specific loneliness of knowing you were the one in charge. Nobody talks about that part. We package failure into lessons, into pivot stories, into the heroic before-shot of a success narrative. But sometimes failure is just failure, and it sits with you, and there's no framework that makes it lighter.
>
> Maybe that's okay. Maybe we've been so obsessed with extracting value from every setback that we've skipped the part where you actually feel it (generated by Claude).

PAUSE HERE

Open your personalized workbook on your computer and review the practice exercise, asking

- In what ways does this passage fail to meet the expectations of a business book?

After answering, revise the passage.

Problem with original B:

It's perfectly fine to use a story and personal thoughts (in fact, I encourage it) in a business book, but this story is more theoretical without a clear takeaway or application. A business reader would think, *Okay, so what do I do with that?*

Revised B:

> [First paragraph stays the same]
>
> We carry on with business as usual and don't talk about that part. And if we do, it's packaged as a lesson and we move on quickly. But skipping or diminishing that part has a cost. In my experience coaching executive teams, leaders who rushed past the discomfort repeated the same mistake later. The ones who paused and got honest about their role grew from the experience.
>
> So if you're in the middle of a failure right now, resist the instinct to extract a platitude and move on. Schedule a deliberate debrief—with yourself or your team—and ask not just *what went wrong* but *what did I avoid seeing?* That question is where the real growth lives.

The emotional honesty is still there, but now there's a credibility signal and a concrete action for the reader.

EDITING STEPS

❑ Change any writing that doesn't match the tone of your genre.

❑ Add in any necessary genre expectations you're missing.

- (Note: You don't necessarily need all genre expectations. For example, some how-to books don't lend themselves to visuals, so you wouldn't have to include them. You do want to include most, if not all, the expectations.)

❑ Rewrite or change the genre if your book doesn't fulfill the genre promise.

❑ Rewrite any passages that don't meet the tone for the genre.

❑ Look for opportunities to speak directly to your target audience and address their specific needs.

❑ Trim or delete information your target audience already knows so the content stays focused and engaging.

❑ Revise or delete any sections that feel off-genre or too advanced/basic for your audience.

STOP: DON'T READ AHEAD YET

Apply the two or three topics you chose for this pass to your manuscript before moving on.

This book is a toolbox, not a linear book. You'll get the most value from doing the work as you go.

If you haven't done so yet, scan the QR code or visit https://beaconpointservices.org/nonfiction-editing -workbook to generate your personalized workbook for the content pass.

When you're ready, come back and begin the next pass.

You've got this.

ORGANIZATION PASS

Pearl S. Buck, a renowned author, said, "Order is the shape upon which beauty depends."[7] Your readers rely on order too. You can have the most beautiful content in the world, but disorganization will make it hard for readers to appreciate. Unless you're Picasso—he could put an eye where the ear should be and still create a masterpiece. But your nonfiction book isn't a Cubist painting, and your reader isn't standing in a museum trying to decode it. Your readers need clarity and logical order.

Now that you've strengthened your content, the *what*, take a minute to reflect on how your content improved to motivate you to keep going. Now you'll focus on the first *how*: how your ideas flow and connect. When I developmentally edit, I handle content and organization together because they're closely linked. But for your self-editing, separate them—one pass for content, another for organization. Separating the passes allows you to focus on one type of issue at a time and only look at what you need to for that topic. You don't necessarily need to read your whole book during this pass.

If your manuscript struggles with . . .

Chapters or sections that feel out of order or disconnected:

- Ensure logical order (page 63)

---

7   Pearl S. Buck, *To My Daughters, with Love* (New York: John Day Company, 1964)

- Strengthen or add transitions (page 81)

Dense, hard-to-navigate text without a clear structure:

- Refine headings and subheadings (page 74)
- Ensure effective paragraph breaks (page 88)

Readers saying "I got lost" or "I had to reread that section":

- Ensure logical order (page 63)
- Strengthen or add transitions (page 81)
- Refine headings and subheadings (page 74)

If you're unsure what to pick, sign up to get notified when my diagnostic tool is ready or check out my Manuscript Checkup service, both in appendix A.

Personalized workbook: To generate your customizable organization pass workbook, scan the QR code or visit https://beaconpointservices.org/nonfiction-editing-workbook.

For best results, open on a computer or tablet to download and edit the Word document.

Ensure Logical Order

Chapter order

The way you structure your book influences how well readers remember your material. Studies show that clear organization improves memory. When text is more logically organized, readers can recall information better.[8]

That's why a strong organizational structure matters. Organize your chapters by theme or by progression, depending on your topic. If concepts build on one another, choose a progressive order. Otherwise, group similar themes together. When organizing by theme, consider placing related chapters into sections—though that's not required.

Or combine both approaches, using themed sections with progressive chapter order inside each one.

Original chapter order for a book on launching a freelance business:

1. Finding Your First Clients
2. Setting Your Rates
3. Defining Your Services
4. Creating a Portfolio
5. Managing Client Relationships
6. Handling Difficult Clients

---

8   Bonnie J. F. Meyer, "Identification of the Structure of Prose and Its Implications for the Study of Reading and Memory," *Journal of Reading Behavior* 7, no. 1 (1975): 7-47, https://doi.org/10.1080/10862967509547120.

7. Building Your Online Presence
8. Scaling Your Business
9. Setting Up Your Business Legally
10. Managing Your Finances

The chapters jump around without a clear pattern. Readers must define their services and establish their legal setup before they look for clients or set rates. Plus, the two client relationship chapters are separated as well, disrupting flow. Essentially, the order doesn't follow a progressive or thematic grouping.

Revised #1. Use a progressive structure (reorder so each chapter builds on the previous):

1. Defining Your Services
2. Setting Up Your Business Legally
3. Setting Your Rates
4. Creating a Portfolio
5. Building Your Online Presence
6. Finding Your First Clients
7. Managing Client Relationships
8. Handling Difficult Clients
9. Managing Your Finances
10. Scaling Your Business

Revised #2. Could use thematic sections with the progressive order:

- Section 1: Foundation
  - Chapter 1: Defining Your Services
  - Chapter 2: Setting Up Your Business Legally
  - Chapter 3: Setting Your Rates
- Section 2: Marketing & Getting Clients
  - Chapter 4: Creating a Portfolio

- o Chapter 5: Building Your Online Presence
  - o Chapter 6: Finding Your First Clients
- Section 3: Working with Clients
  - o Chapter 7: Managing Client Relationships
  - o Chapter 8: Handling Difficult Clients
- Section 4: Business Operations
  - o Chapter 9: Managing Your Finances
  - o Chapter 10: Scaling Your Business

Choosing a structure

It's not always clear whether a progressive or thematic structure is better. If several structures could work, how do you know whether your original one is the best choice?

First, focus on your reader's journey, not just your content. What does your reader need to understand first, and what would confuse them if it appeared in the "wrong" spot? If you can answer that clearly, then problem solved.

When that doesn't solve the issue and both structures work equally well, choose the one that reduces cognitive overload. Is your topic easier to understand through themes or through progression? Go with the easiest to follow.

When all else fails, default to the structure most commonly used for your topic.

Choose a progressive structure when your topic involves

- steps
- processes
- timelines
- cause-and-effect
- building skills

If one concept must come before another, choose progression.

Choose to group by themes when your topic is

- conceptual
- multi-faceted
- non-linear
- principle-based
- something readers may want to skim or return to

If your reader doesn't need a strict path, themes give you more flexibility.

If both structures work, combine them: Use thematic sections with progressive chapters inside each one. This works well for some business, self-help, or productivity books.

And, honestly, sometimes chapter A could follow chapter B, but if you can create a smoother transition by having A first, go with that. Strong transitions make reading easier. So when the order doesn't matter, then look to what makes for a better transition or lead-in to the next.

Content order

All content in a given chapter should align with that chapter's main topic, and the material under each heading should clearly support that heading. If it doesn't, move it to where it fits more naturally, either somewhere else in the chapter or another chapter entirely.

Original section in a chapter titled "Creating Your Content Calendar":

Planning Your Social Media Posts

A content calendar helps you stay consistent with your social media presence without scrambling for ideas every day.

[Continued information about content pillars and batching content]

When writing your captions, keep your ideal client in mind. Use language that resonates with them and addresses their pain points. Make sure you have clear, compelling messaging so they understand the value you offer. Strong messaging is what converts followers into clients.

Also consider what times your audience is most active. Check your analytics to see when your posts get the most engagement, then schedule your content for those peak windows.

The paragraph about captions and converting followers is off topic for this heading. This section should stay focused on the logistics of planning posts, not on messaging strategy.

Revised:

Move the messaging paragraph to a section about brand voice (ideally earlier in the chapter, before the content-planning material).

Just like your chapter order, your headings should follow either a thematic or progressive structure.

Example chapters on building your email list:

- Writing Welcome Emails
- Choosing an Email Service Provider
- Setting Up Automation
- Creating Your Lead Magnet
- Designing Your Opt-In Form
- Writing Your Landing Page Copy

The order doesn't follow a logical progression. You can't write welcome emails before choosing an email platform or creating the lead magnet that readers will sign up for. And automation only comes after you have designed the opt-in form.

New order:

- Creating Your Lead Magnet
- Choosing an Email Service Provider
- Designing Your Opt-In Form
- Writing Your Landing Page Copy
- Setting Up Automation
- Writing Welcome Emails

> **Complexity note**
>
> Because this topic spans the entire book, this practice section is longer than usual. Tackle the changes you would make to the chapter order and content order as best you can. Then use my example to help you further understand this topic. After the revision, I explained the overall changes I made. Because this example is already long, I didn't explain each and every change, but enough to give you an idea.

Self-editing in practice

This is the original order of a book on creating a Kickstarter that I edited. To shorten it, I removed most of the subheadings from the outline and left only the ones needed to practice the concept.

Original:

Chapter 1: Put Together a Launch Team
- Email
- Private Facebook Groups
- Public Facebook Page
- Stay in Contact

- Make the Ask

Chapter 2: Reaching Out to Your Network

Chapter 3: Publicity

Chapter 4: Reward Levels

Chapter 5: Running the Numbers

- Phases (from idea to ready to go)
- The Video
- Promotions
- Vendors
- Calculate Your Kickstarter Goal

Chapter 6: Campaign Descriptions

Chapter 7: Preparing for Launch

Chapter 8: Post Campaign

Chapter 9: When Things Go Wrong

Chapter 10: Stretch Goal

PAUSE HERE

Open your personalized workbook on your computer and review the practice exercise, asking

- Which chapters or sections feel like they belong earlier, later, or together in a group?

- Do any headings or subheadings seem out of place for the chapter they're in, or unrelated to the main idea?

After answering, draft a revised order and compare it to mine.

Problems with original:

The first three chapters follow a clear progression. Chapters 4–6, however, don't follow any thematic or progressive order. Chapters 7–9 return to a progressive structure, while chapter 10 is randomly thrown in.

Chapter 5 ("Running the Numbers") ran long, and several sections drifted from the core idea of running the numbers. Many were off topic for this chapter.

One section in chapter 1 doesn't relate to that chapter. And some subheadings appeared out of sequence.

Revised order (Again, to keep it short, I left out some of the less relevant subheadings):

Section 1: Where Are You At?
- Chapter 1: Phases

Section 2: Marketing and Promoting
- Chapter 2: Putting Together a Launch Team
  - Ask People to Join Your Launch Team
  - Choose a Platform
    - Email
    - Private Facebook Groups
  - Stay in Contact
- Chapter 3: Public Facebook Page
- Chapter 4: Reaching Out to Your Network
- Chapter 5: Publicity

Section 3: Putting Your Campaign Together
- Chapter 6: Reward Levels
- Chapter 7: Stretch Goals
- Chapter 8: The Video
- Chapter 9: Campaign Descriptions

Section 4: Calculating Costs and Working with Vendors
- Chapter 10: Vendors
- Chapter 11: Running the Numbers
  - Promotions
  - Calculate Your Kickstarter Goal
  - Price Your Rewards

Section 5: Preparing for Launch

- Chapter 12: It's Launch Time

Section 6: Post Campaign

- Chapter 13: If You Didn't Reach Your Goal
- Chapter 14: If You Reached Your Goal
- Chapter 15: When Things Go Wrong

SUMMARY OF CHANGES

Moved the phases to a new chapter 1

Problem: The "phases" content was buried in chapter 5 even though it explains the basic stages every Kickstarter goes through.

Solution: Made it chapter 1 because readers need this foundation before learning marketing tactics.

Minor tweaks to the original progressive order

Problem: Chapters 1 through 3 in the original manuscript followed a logical, progressive order, but not all the subheadings fit.

Solution: I grouped them under a new section called *Marketing and Promoting the Kickstarter Campaign* to give thematic clarity. Then I added in level 2 headings to nest similar content in level 3 headings. (Choose a Platform → new heading to nest "email" and "private Facebook group" to see how they relate instead of keeping them as different topics). Pulled out the public Facebook section into its own chapter since it didn't relate to the launch team content.

Creating thematic cohesion

Problem: Related chapters were scattered (e.g., reward levels in chapter 4, stretch goals in chapter 10, campaign descriptions in chapter 6), and unrelated content was thrown together in chapter 5.

Solution: Created thematic sections and moved chapters and unrelated content in chapter 5 according to the new themed sections.

(e.g., grouped all campaign creation topics in section 3: Putting Your Campaign Together).

Rearranging unrelated content

Problem: Chapter 5 contained phases, video creation, vendor information, promotions, and budget calculations—completely unrelated topics.

Solution: Distributed content to appropriate thematic homes:

- Phases → became the foundation (Chapter 1)
- Video → became its own chapter and moved to section 3 (putting campaign together)
- Vendors and budget calculations → became their own chapters in section 4 (Calculating Costs. Working with Vendors.)

To improve flow, I reversed the order of the vendor and budgeting content—readers need to know their vendor costs before they can accurately calculate their campaign budget.

Used both thematic and progressive order

Problem: Original chapters had no clear relationship to each other.

Solution: Grouped related chapters in sections, and within each section, chapters follow a logical sequence (like moving from finding vendors to calculating costs).

EDITING STEPS

❑ Examine each chapter in context and ask, "Does this chapter belong in this spot? Is it thematically grouped or part of a natural sequence?" If not, and multiple aren't, figure out whether to group them by theme or progression and reorganize them.

❑ Examine each chapter in context and ask, "Would the transition work better between these chapters if the order was switched?" If so, then flip the chapter order.

❑ Check that every paragraph aligns with the chapter's overall topic. Flag it if it doesn't.

❑ Check that all content under a given heading relates to that heading's focus. Flag it if it doesn't.

❑ Review all headings within a chapter and ask if each one is in the right spot progressively or thematically. Flag misplaced headings.

❑ Review all flagged items and delete anything redundant or off topic, or move it to a more fitting chapter or section.

Refine Headings and Subheadings

You may have opened a nonfiction book and encountered a chapter with seventeen subheadings, each only two paragraphs long. By the third page, you're exhausted from all the stopping and starting, wondering if you're reading a book or a poorly organized filing cabinet. I have.

Yes, headings and subheadings help with organization, but too many overwhelm readers, and too few leave them wandering. Not every nonfiction book needs headings and subheadings, but most could benefit from them. Headings are a quick way to transition between significant ideas. Sure, you could write a transition, but that often adds unnecessary length and slows the reading experience.

No one wants to wade through long explanations about how ideas connect before reaching the next point. So headings help! But do use transitions between subtopics (see transition editing topic on page 81) instead of nesting more headings when they're unnecessary.

Consistency

Consistency doesn't mean every chapter must use headings or that none can. It simply means using them in a way that feels coherent. If only one chapter doesn't need headings, consider making it a subsection. A single outlier often feels awkward, as readers get used to the book's format. However, you can have a few chapters without any headings in a book where several chapters do have headings. So don't put headings in a chapter that doesn't need them just because other chapters have them.

This applies to the levels as well. If only one chapter goes four levels deep with subheadings, see if you really need that fourth-level heading. But you can have some chapters go three levels deep and some only go two levels and/or one level deep.

Right amount of headings

You don't need a heading, no matter how clever and cute, to separate paragraphs covering the same idea. While each paragraph introduces a slightly new idea, reserve subheadings for major shifts.

In a book on creating a Kickstarter, the chapter on putting together a launch team used the heading "Email" with nested headings on related email topics. This structure would work if each topic had depth, but with only a paragraph per topic, the headings were unnecessary so added clutter rather than clarity.

Sometimes you have to add a heading to group like-content together. I added a new heading, "Choose a Platform," because the original structure was misleading. Without that heading, the structure implied the author wanted readers to use both email and a private Facebook page since they were both level-one subheadings. In reality, the author offered pros, cons, and tips for each method, so I created the subheading "Choose a Platform" to group them properly.

(I also moved "Make the Ask" earlier for logical flow and removed "Public Facebook Page" since it was off topic, but we're focusing on the number of headings, not order.)

The original:	Edited version:

Put Together a Launch Team
• Email
  ○ Why choose email
  ○ How to make email entertaining
  ○ Email length
• Private Facebook Groups
• Public Facebook Page
• Stay in Contact
• Make the Ask
	Put Together a Launch Team
	• Ask People to Join Your Launch Team
	• Choose a Platform
	  ○ Email
	  ○ Private Facebook Page
	• Stay in Contact

Now, let's look at another example from that book. In the publicity chapter, the author discussed finding and building relationships with influencers before introducing any headings. Having content before the first heading is fine and actually preferable—introductory material often belongs there. But because the author used headings for two types of publicity (local publicity and Kickstarter promotions), it made sense to add a heading for influencers as well.

Original subheadings in the publicity chapter:	Edited version:

Content about finding and building a relationship with influencers before any headings.
 	
• Local Publicity
• Local Radio/TV Shows
  ○ The pitch
• Kickstarter Promotions
• Where We Went Wrong
	• Local Publicity
	  ○ Radio/TV
	  ○ Make the pitch
	• Connecting with Influencers
	  ○ Finding them
	  ○ Building a relationship with them
	  ○ Making the pitch
	• Kickstarter Promotions
	• Where We Went Wrong

Heading levels

Nest headings appropriately. If content underneath a given heading strongly relates to content under the previous heading, you may consider nesting it. In our example publicity chapter, the author had these two headings assigned the same level:

- Local Publicity
- Local Radio/TV Shows

Since local radio/TV shows are a type of local publicity, it makes more sense to nest the second one.

As mentioned earlier, if you find yourself nesting deeper than you have in previous chapters, question whether you need the heading at all.

Self-editing in practice

As you read, note any headings that clutter the flow, any that belong as subheadings, and any places where adding a heading would guide readers more effectively.

Original (I listed the headings and then briefly described the content found under each heading):

Chapter Title: Building and Using Your Author Brand

<u>Branding Basics</u>

Explaining the importance of branding and everything it includes.

<u>Voice and Tone</u>

Knowing your genre helps you define your author identity. Are you a cozy mystery writer or a dark sci-fi author? Your genre shapes your brand tone and visuals. Your voice should sound like you. Formal, funny, quirky—own it. That way your brand feels natural.

<u>Visual Branding</u>

Choose colors and fonts that reflect your genre and vibe. You don't have to hire a designer, but try to keep things polished.

<u>Social Media</u>

Why you should use social media and how it helps build your brand.

<u>Which platform is best for you?</u>

There's no one-size-fits-all. Writers of fantasy might find a strong community on Instagram or Discord, while business writers may get better results from LinkedIn. Your brand voice might fit better on Instagram than LinkedIn.

<u>Email Lists</u>

Email lists help you stay connected to readers. You "own" your list, unlike social media platforms.

<u>What to send</u>

Choosing on-brand information to send. Emails can include updates, sneak peeks, or writing tips—whatever fits your brand and serves your readers.

<u>Make it personal</u>

Let your personality shine. Readers want to know the person behind the pen.

PAUSE HERE

Open your personalized workbook on your computer and review the practice exercise, asking

- Do any headings feel unnecessary—like they're just labeling a short paragraph that could flow without a break?

- Do several headings clearly belong under one larger idea instead of all sitting at the same level?

- Does anything feel like it needs a heading to signal a major shift in topic but doesn't have one yet?

After answering, edit the headings and subheadings before seeing mine.

Revised headings and subheadings (showing them side-by-side for easier comparison)

Original	Revised	Explanation
Branding Basics		*Deleted this heading. This section contained introductory material for the chapter, so can come after chapter title. Doesn't need a separate heading.
Voice and Tone Visual Branding Social Media • Which platform is best for you Email Lists • What to send • Make it personal	Building Your Brand • Define your genre • Voice and tone • Visual branding Using Your Brand with Content Marketing • Social media • Email lists	Added "Building Your Brand" to group like-content. Since several of the original main headings were about building your brand, I grouped and nested them.) • Added "define your genre" because the original voice and tone section covered genre and voice and tone, so there were two topics there so needed another heading, nested) • Voice and tone (same, just nested) • Visual branding (same, just nested) Added "Using Your Brand with Content Marketing" to group like-content • Social media (same, just nested and deleted the "which platform is best for you" that was originally nested under social media) • Email lists (same, just nested)

EDITING STEPS

❑ Check for outlier chapters that either don't use headings or go deeper in nesting than others. If only one chapter breaks the pattern, revise it for consistency.

❑ Delete unnecessary headings and subheadings (especially those that separate short, related paragraphs that could easily flow together with a transition).

❑ Add necessary headings to break up long stretches of text or to clarify major topic shifts.

❑ Nest heading levels logically, where subtopics clearly belong under a larger idea.

Strengthen or Add Transitions

Lack of transitions bothers me—maybe because my brain already feels scrambled, so I don't enjoy chaotic text. I need bridges, and while I may get a little overzealous about transitions, I promise that readers appreciate them even if they don't notice.

When writers jump from one idea to the next without showing the connection, the result feels scattered. Yes, your readers can eventually determine the connection **after** they read both ideas, but you want the reader to understand it **as** they read the new idea.

Often I'll leave a query asking how the new idea connects to the previous one, only to discover the answer several paragraphs—or even pages—later. In those cases, I go back and delete the query and add the needed transition. Other times, the query stays because the relationship never becomes clear.

Tips for effective transitions

Transition words like "next," "additionally," "furthermore," "however," etc. aren't effective transitions between two full ideas. Those transitions work at the sentence level, even sometimes at the paragraph level, but never on a content level. If several paragraphs in a row expand on the same idea, then those transitional words work. But once you move to a new idea, you need a stronger transition. An effective transition clarifies the relationship between the ideas.

> **Caveat**
>
> Subheadings and headings can replace the need for a transition since the new heading signals the shift. However, it wouldn't hurt to have one. But as mentioned in the Refine headings and subheadings lesson, you don't want too many headings, and that's where transitions come in.

Use this formula for an effective transition: Mention the old, bring in the new, and add a connecting statement.

The connection can appear anywhere in your transition—just ensure the old idea comes before the new one.

Example transitions

Original:

> Old idea: People and culprits in your life that can keep you from dating effectively.
>
> New idea: You must determine why you want to date.

Right after describing the last culprit, the author added a sentence that felt unrelated: "As with all things in your life, you must determine your why: why do you want to date?"

Um . . . what? What does that have to do with culprits?

Revised:

> After you eliminate the culprit(s) in your life, take a look at your-
> self. What if you are the culprit? If your reason for dating isn't a
> good one, you may be preventing yourself from effective dating.

> *Formula: Mention the old topic (culprits), introduce the new topic (rea-
> son for dating), and add a connecting statement (the second happens after
> the first; the second topic may be another aspect of the first; and both
> ensure you're dating effectively)*

Original:

> Old topic: The community should care more about food allergies.

> New topic: The second time my son had an incident.

Revised:

> While I hoped others would understand food allergies and adapt
> to our culture, I don't regret choosing to allow [name] to brave
> the world so both he and I could feel normal, connected, and
> involved. But it did result in another incident. However, this time
> we kept him safe for a longer duration.

> *Formula: Mention the old topic (community understanding), introduce
> the new topic (second instance), and add a connecting statement (she
> doesn't regret the old topic even though it led to the new topic)*

Self-editing in practice

Original A:

For years, the hustle culture mindset has dominated the conversation around success. We're told to wake up earlier, work longer, and squeeze productivity into every available moment. Social media praises entrepreneurs who never take a day off and celebrates the "no excuses" mentality. But this constant pressure to perform can lead to exhaustion, resentment, and ultimately, burnout.

Even when we love our work, we can stay in hustle mode for too long. We begin to feel guilty during moments of rest. Our self-worth becomes tangled in how much we accomplish. And instead of feeling empowered, we start feeling trapped by our own drive. Eventually, motivation declines.

Rest isn't a reward for finishing your to-do list—it's a requirement for doing good work. When we build recovery into our routines, we're not slacking; we're honoring the natural ebb and flow of energy. Athletes understand this. They don't train at full intensity every day. They rest strategically to improve performance and avoid injury.

The same principle applies to mental and emotional labor. Breaks allow us to return with renewed focus, fresh ideas, and stronger resilience. Whether it's taking a walk, scheduling a no-work weekend, or setting boundaries around your time, intentional rest is one of the most powerful tools for sustainable productivity (generated by ChatGPT).

PAUSE HERE

Open your personalized workbook on your computer and review the practice exercise, asking

- Where does the passage shift from one idea or focus to another?

After answering, draft a transition between those topics following the formula, then check my revision.

Problem with original A:

This starts off discussing the problem with hustle culture, then moves into the importance of intentional rest and recovery. The topics work in the same chapter, but they need a transition to connect them.

Revised A:

> This decline likely means that your mind and body need a break. You need to give them that break and rest they deserve, not push harder.

> *This added transition could go either at the end of paragraph 2 or start of paragraph 3.*

Original B:

> Launching a digital product is exciting, but many writers rush it. They create a course or workbook, put it on their website, and hope people will just find it. Then, when sales don't come in, they assume the offer isn't good. In reality, the problem is usually that not enough people knew it existed in the first place. Visibility—not value—is the missing piece.

Social media is one of the best ways to learn what your audience actually cares about. Posting consistently gives you real-time feedback on which topics get attention. You can test headlines, hooks, and angles before you ever build your product. And once you have the product, social platforms help you stay in front of people so they remember to buy (generated by ChatGPT).

PAUSE HERE

Open your personalized workbook on your computer and review the practice exercise, asking

- Where does the passage shift from one idea or focus to another?

After answering, draft a transition between those topics following the formula, then check my revision.

Problem with original B:

The first paragraph discusses why digital products don't sell. The second paragraph jumps to using social media to test and warm your audience.

Revised B:

You can get that visibility through social media, a place where you can warm people up and let them see, react to, and remember your offer.

This added transition could go either at the end of paragraph 1 or start of paragraph 2.

EDITING STEPS

❏ Pause whenever you switch to a new idea (Identify where your topic or focus shifts, even slightly.)

❏ Ask, "Does the transition contain a clear relationship between the ideas up front before readers get too deep into the new topic?"

❏ If not or if you don't even have a transition, write or rewrite one using the transition formula: Mention the old topic → introduce the new topic → show the connection.

Ensure Effective Paragraph Breaks

Research confirms what readers already feel: Well-chunked text is easier to process and remember, while dense, unbroken paragraphs make the brain work harder than it needs to.[9] I'm sure you can recall a time you've opened a book or an article online and been met with a massive block of text that made your eyes glaze over before you even started reading. I have. I immediately think, *Do I really want to read this?* And sometimes I don't. That's the power—or danger—of paragraph breaks.

While paragraph breaks have always mattered, one can argue they matter even more now that we live in a world of skimmers. Even readers who plan to read every word will scan first to see if your book looks approachable.

Paragraph breaks give your readers visual breathing room and help you organize your ideas so they're easy to follow. This means don't just randomly decide to press Enter whenever. The break should be intentional. When done well, they guide readers through your content without them even noticing. When done poorly, they create walls of text that feel exhausting to scale.

---

9   Dongping Liu, "The Effects of Segmentation on Cognitive Load, Vocabulary Learning and Retention, and Reading Comprehension in a Multimedia Learning Environment," BMC Psychology 12, no. 1 (January 2, 2024): 4, https://doi.org/10.1186/s40359-023-01489-5.

Guidelines for effective paragraph breaks

ONE MAIN IDEA PER PARAGRAPH

Each paragraph should develop one main point. It can contain supporting details, but everything must tie to that one main idea. When you transition into a new subtopic or a different angle on the current topic, start a new paragraph. This keeps your writing focused and prevents readers from getting confused about what you're trying to say.

If you're not sure if a sentence belongs, ask, "How closely is this tied to the previous sentence?" If your readers should view both sentences together, it should stay in the same paragraph.

Original:

> Many first-time authors underestimate how much time revision actually takes. They assume the first draft will only need minor tweaks before it's ready for readers. But strong writing rarely appears fully formed on the first attempt. Most professional authors expect to revise multiple times before a manuscript is truly polished. A structured editing process helps you tackle those revisions in manageable stages without the overwhelm. Instead of trying to fix everything at once, focus on one type of improvement at a time. One pass might strengthen your ideas, another might reorganize sections for better flow, and another might tighten your writing. Breaking revision into stages makes the process clearer, faster, and far less intimidating.

The paragraph discusses how revision takes longer than writers expect, and then it switches to how to manage revision. That's a new angle.

Revised:

Many first-time authors underestimate how much time revision actually takes. They assume the first draft will only need minor tweaks before it's ready for readers. But strong writing rarely appears fully formed on the first attempt. Most professional authors expect to revise multiple times before a manuscript is truly polished.

A structured editing process helps you tackle those revisions in manageable stages without the overwhelm. Instead of trying to fix everything at once, focus on one type of improvement at a time. One pass might strengthen your ideas, another might reorganize sections for better flow, and another might tighten your writing. Breaking revision into stages makes the process clearer, faster, and far less intimidating.

Example:

Many nonfiction authors try to sound overly formal because they believe it makes them look more credible. They load their writing with long sentences, complex phrasing, and academic vocabulary. Ironically, this often makes their ideas harder to understand and less persuasive to everyday readers. Clear writing builds trust faster than impressive-sounding language ever will.

The final sentence could technically start a new paragraph because it's a subtle shift from common mistakes to the importance of clarity. But it directly reinforces the point of the paragraph—that overly formal writing hurts clarity—so keeping it together strengthens the argument.

BREAK UP WALLS OF TEXT

If a paragraph runs longer than 150–200 words (roughly 8–10 lines in a standard book format), determine if there's a natural place to break it. Not every long paragraph needs to be split, but if you have several in a row, your reader will feel it. This is worth repeating: You don't need to split up a paragraph just because it's over the ideal word count. Just take a closer look and see if it would better serve the reader if it were separated.

For narrative sections (like stories or anecdotes), longer paragraphs work. For instructional content (like how-to steps), keep them shorter.

VARY PARAGRAPH LENGTH

Just like you vary sentence length for rhythm, vary your paragraph length for visual interest and pacing. A mix of short, medium, and occasional longer paragraphs keeps the reader engaged.

Short paragraphs (one to three sentences) work well for:

- Emphasis
- Transitions between major ideas
- Punchy statements that need to land
- Dialogue in anecdotes

Medium paragraphs (four to seven sentences) work well for:

- Explaining concepts
- Providing examples
- Building an argument

Longer paragraphs (eight or more sentences) work well for:

- Complex explanations that need to stay together
- Detailed stories or case studies
- When breaking would disrupt the flow

USE SINGLE-SENTENCE PARAGRAPHS STRATEGICALLY

A one-sentence paragraph draws attention, so it can be used for dramatic effect: when you want something to really land—a key takeaway, a turning point in a story, or a transition to a new section. But don't overdo it. If every third paragraph is a single sentence, the effect loses its power. Save it for moments that truly deserve emphasis.

Example:

> Many nonfiction authors focus so much on explaining their ideas that they forget the reader's experience. They pile on facts and explanations, believing more information automatically means more value. But more information doesn't lead to more engagement. Readers stay engaged because the ideas are clear and easy to follow.
>
> Clarity beats complexity every time.
>
> When readers understand your message quickly, they're far more likely to trust you and keep reading. . . .

That one-sentence paragraph in between two longer ones gives it emphasis. To keep the example short, I didn't put in the last paragraph in full, but it would continue for several more sentences.

WATCH FOR "FALSE PARAGRAPHS"

Sometimes writers break a paragraph in the middle of explaining a single idea just because it "looks long." But if the content is still developing the same point, breaking it can actually confuse readers.

Ask, Does this new paragraph introduce a new idea, or am I still explaining the previous one? If you're still on the same idea, keep it together or find a way to tighten the writing instead of arbitrarily splitting it.

Example:

> Strong introductions help readers understand what they're about to learn and why it matters. They give context, clarify the problem the book will address, and set expectations for what the reader will gain. Without that foundation, readers may struggle to see how the information connects to their goals.
>
> That's why effective introductions often include a brief roadmap of the book. This preview shows readers how the chapters fit together and reassures them that the author has a clear plan for guiding them through the material.

The roadmap explanation isn't a new topic, as it's still developing the same point—what makes introductions effective—so splitting the paragraph weakens the flow instead of improving readability.

Self-editing in practice

Original:

> Building a strong morning routine can transform your entire day, but it doesn't happen by accident. You need to be intentional about the habits you're creating and realistic about what you can actually maintain long-term. Many people try to overhaul their entire morning at once—waking up two hours earlier, adding meditation, exercise, journaling, and an elaborate breakfast routine—only to burn out within a week. The key is to start small and build gradually. Maybe you begin with just drinking a glass of water when you wake up. That's it. One simple habit that takes thirty seconds. Once that feels automatic, you add something else. Maybe a five-minute stretch or writing down three things

you're grateful for. The goal isn't to create an Instagram-worthy morning routine that looks impressive. Instead, you want your routine to actually serve you and be easy to stick with when life gets messy. And life will get messy. Some mornings you will hit snooze —when your kid is sick, when you have an early meeting, when you just don't feel like it. Your routine needs to be flexible enough to adapt without falling apart completely. This is why starting small matters. If your entire routine hinges on waking up at 5 a.m., what happens when you can't? But if your routine is built on small, stackable habits, you can still do some of them even on chaotic mornings. You might not get your full workout in, but you can still drink that glass of water and take three deep breaths. That continuity matters more than perfection.

PAUSE HERE

Open your personalized workbook on your computer and review the practice exercise, asking

- Where does the passage shift from one main idea to another?

- Which sections feel dense or overwhelming and would benefit from visual breathing room?

- Are there any sentences that deserve emphasis and would be stronger as their own paragraph?

After answering, revise the passage to improve paragraph breaks before checking my revision.

Problem with original:

This is one massive 262-word paragraph that covers multiple distinct ideas. Each of these deserves its own paragraph.

Revised:

> Building a strong morning routine can transform your entire day, but it doesn't happen by accident. You need to be intentional about the habits you're creating and realistic about what you can actually maintain long-term.
>
> Many people try to overhaul their entire morning at once—waking up two hours earlier, adding meditation, exercise, journaling, and an elaborate breakfast routine—only to burn out within a week. The key is to start small and build gradually. Maybe you begin with just drinking a glass of water when you wake up. That's it. One simple habit that takes thirty seconds. Once that feels automatic, you add something else. Maybe a five-minute stretch or writing down three things you're grateful for.
>
> The goal isn't to create an Instagram-worthy morning routine that looks impressive. Instead, you want your routine to actually serve you and be easy to stick with when life gets messy. And life will get messy. Some mornings you will hit snooze, when your kid is sick, when you have an early meeting, when you just don't feel like it. Your routine needs to be flexible enough to adapt without falling apart completely.
>
> This is why starting small matters. If your entire routine hinges on waking up at 5 a.m., what happens when you can't? But if your routine is built on small, stackable habits, you can still do some of them even on chaotic mornings. You might not get your full workout in, but you can still drink that glass of water and take three deep breaths.

That continuity matters more than perfection.

I broke the original into five paragraphs. I opted to have the last one be a one-sentence paragraph for emphasis; however, it could have been the last sentence of the fourth paragraph.

Each paragraph break happened with a topic switch: 1st paragraph = creating it intentionally, 2nd paragraph = problem with overhauling and how to start small (notice I wrote two topics here. That's fine because it's still one focus: the problem and how to fix it, and the ideas were short), 3rd paragraph = importance of flexibility, 4th paragraph = how to start small. Then I ended with an emphasis statement.

EDITING STEPS

❑ Highlight any paragraph that runs longer than 150–200 words (8–10 lines in your book format). Ask, Does this long paragraph contain multiple distinct ideas? If yes, look for natural breaking points where the focus shifts. If not, keep it as is.

❑ Check for variety: Do you have a mix of short, medium, and longer paragraphs, or are they all roughly the same length?

❑ Look for moments that deserve emphasis. Could a key statement land harder as a single-sentence paragraph?

❑ If you've included dialogue or conversations in your anecdotes, make sure you're breaking for each new speaker.

❑ Scan for areas with several short paragraphs in a row and ensure each paragraph is introducing a new idea rather than just breaking up a paragraph that was split only because it looked too long.

  • Put paragraphs together that belong together.

STOP: DON'T READ AHEAD YET

Apply the two or three topics you chose for this pass to your manuscript before moving on.

This book is a toolbox, not a linear book. You'll get the most value from doing the work as you go.

If you haven't done so yet, scan the QR code or visit https://beaconpointservices.org/nonfiction-editing -workbook to generate your personalized workbook for the organization pass.

When you're ready, come back and begin the next pass.

You've got this.

WRITING PASS

Most readers decide within *seconds* whether they trust an author's voice, and your sentences form the foundation of that credibility. In one manuscript I edited, nearly every sentence was wordier than necessary. When the author received my edited file, he said, "Thanks for making me look smart," and then immediately asked, "Do you think I have a good book? There were a lot of edits."

Yes, he had a great book, full of solid, insightful content. The ideas were just buried under unwieldy sentences that obscured the message. Once I tightened the writing, his brilliance finally had room to breathe.

In this pass, you'll focus on the second *how*: how the manuscript is written, ensuring your prose is clear, sharp, precise, and engaging.

Read your manuscript aloud while doing this. I say read, but you actually want to *hear* your manuscript read aloud to you. When you read silently, your brain autocorrects mistakes and fills in gaps without your realizing it. But when you hear the words, you process them differently. Your auditory system catches awkward phrasing, repetitive words, and clunky sentences that your eyes skipped right over. You'll notice where you stumble, where sentences run too long, and where the rhythm feels off.

If you have a friend willing to read aloud to you, introduce me; they're a keeper. For the sake of saving your friendships, just use your computer's built-in text-to-speech software. If you're really fancy, buy an app.

As always, choose only two or three topics to focus on.

If you're unsure what to pick, sign up to get notified when my diagnostic tool is ready or check out my Manuscript Checkup service, both in appendix A.

Topics to choose from:

- Ensure good sentence fluency (page 100)
- Eliminate excess "be" verbs (page 111)
- Reduce wordiness (page 118)
- Maintain consistent tone (page 125)
- Ensure accurate reading level (page 130)

Personalized workbook: To generate your customizable writing pass workbook, scan the QR code or visit https://beaconpointservices.org/nonfiction-editing-workbook.

For best results, open on a computer or tablet to download and edit the Word document.

Ensure Good Sentence Fluency

Remember the "dry eyes" guy? The "Bueller" guy? Same guy. Look, his signature deadpan delivery may be funny, but it wouldn't work in writing. That lack of variety would decrease the narrative's fluidity if translated to text.

To increase your manuscript's fluidity, ensure sentence variety. This means varying your sentence beginnings, length, and type. Such variety prevents monotony and repetitive rhythms.

Example:

> Sarah developed a plan to restructure the team. Kevin led the first training session. The company introduced a new project management tool. Several managers asked for additional support. One intern created a resource guide for the onboarding process. Leadership approved all the changes by the end of the week.

Each sentence starts with the subject, follows a similar length, and relies on simple sentences.

Monotony can also exist when you vary some sentence elements but not others.

Vary sentence beginnings

Make sure your sentences start in different ways. Of course, don't start too many sentences in a row with the same word, but notice I said the same *way*, not the same *word*. In your manuscript, you likely will begin several sentences in a row the same way—it's a lengthy document, after all. But when a section doesn't flow well, reads flat, or has a repetitive rhythm, varying sentence beginnings can fix that.

SENTENCE PATTERN 1: BEGIN WITH THE SUBJECT

The most common sentence pattern starts with the subject (who or what the sentence is about).

> **My daughter** loves to spin in circles.

> **This story** is driving me nuts.

SENTENCE PATTERN 2: BEGIN WITH A PREPOSITIONAL PHRASE

A preposition shows direction, location, or time.

> **Over on the other side of the bridge**, I saw a lone man walking toward me.

> **Along the way**, we learn a lot of great life lessons.

SENTENCE PATTERN 3: BEGIN WITH A PARTICIPLE OR PARTICIPIAL PHRASE

A participle is a verb that ends in –ing or –ed.

Feeling a little tired, I had put my tablet aside and started to doze off when my cat jumped on me, reminding me to get to work.

Wracked with sorrow, I left without saying a word.

> ### Problems to avoid
>
> When you use sentence pattern 3, watch out for dangling modifiers: *Walking to work, a police car whizzed by.* This makes it sound like the police car was the one walking. After the participial phrase, the subject (the doer) should come first.
>
> You also need to watch out for creating false simultaneity: *Getting up out of the chair, he walked to the front door.* These actions can't both happen at the same time.

SENTENCE PATTERN 4: BEGIN WITH A DEPENDENT CLAUSE

A dependent clause starts with a subordinating conjunction, a connecting word that bridges the complete sentence to the partial sentence.

Because it rained, we had to cancel the party.

While I was taking the test, my pen ran out of ink.

SENTENCE PATTERN 5: BEGIN WITH AN APPOSITIVE

An appositive is a noun phrase that describes another noun.

A well-respected mayor, Bill knew he could run for president.

A struggling magician, Tom wandered from street to street.

SENTENCE PATTERN 6: BEGIN WITH AN INFINITIVE PHRASE

An infinitive is the word "to" plus a verb.

> **To be successful**, I had to start spending some money and investing in this.

> **To reduce my social media time**, I blocked Facebook messages from showing up on my phone.

SENTENCE PATTERN 7: BEGIN WITH A SINGLE-WORD MODIFIER

A single-word modifier is one word that modifies the meaning of a word, clause, or phrase.

> **Happily,** she skipped to her room.

If you use the same sentence-beginning pattern too many times in a row, it can make your narrative feel monotonous.

Original (From a manuscript I edited with names changed):

> "I knew that sweet and loving man was still there somewhere. He was just hiding behind the walls he had built around his heart. I knew that me leaving for Maui had hurt him deeply. That is why he had built the walls in the first place. I felt partially responsible for this. I tried to make it work. He was just too afraid to take the walls down, feel his emotions, and be vulnerable again."

Original contains seven sentences in a row beginning with a subject, and while the lengths vary, they are all simple sentences.

Revised:

> Knowing he was just afraid to be vulnerable again, I tried to make it work. I knew that sweet, loving man was still there somewhere, hiding behind the walls he had built around his heart. Walls he felt he had to build because of me. Despite his inexcusable behavior, I felt partially responsible because I had temporarily left him for Maui.

My revision condensed the seven sentences into four sentences beginning with a participial phrase, subject, subject, and prepositional phrase. It also varies the types.

Original (From a manuscript I edited with names changed):

> "We often turn on ourselves with a defeatist attitude, which is way more prevalent than you'd think. This thinking leads us down a rabbit hole, and many of us wind up giving up because the experience is too painful. Most of us don't have a support system in place at the beginning, making it even more difficult. You need someone near you who can give you a good slap to shake you back to your senses.
>
> "The great news is that it doesn't have to be a painful experience. If you can tell yourself to keep it simple and operate in a realistic fashion, success is there for the taking."

The original contains five sentences in a row beginning with a subject and then one with a dependent clause. The lengths and types are varied, however. Notice how this passage contains multiple paragraphs. You have to check for all sentences in a row, not just ones in the same paragraph.

Revised:

> Sadly, we often turn on ourselves with a defeatist attitude. With this thinking, we enter a deep rabbit hole, causing many of us to give up because the experience brings too much pain, and we don't have a support system in place. You need someone near you who can give you a good slap and shake you back to your senses. Fortunately, this doesn't have to be a painful experience. If you can tell yourself to keep it simple and operate in a realistic fashion, you can achieve success.

In the rewritten version, I varied the sentence beginnings: single-word modifier, prepositional phrase, subject, single-word modifier, and dependent clause.

Sentence length and type

As I mentioned at the start of this lesson, even if you vary your sentence beginnings, you might be using the same sentence type too often.

SIMPLE SENTENCE

A simple sentence is one complete thought.

> The cat slept on the couch.

> My brother and I went to the park and played soccer.

Sentences don't have to begin with the subject to be a simple sentence.

> On the windowsill, the cat naps peacefully.

> Every morning, birds chirp outside my window.

COMPOUND SENTENCE

A compound sentence has two or more complete thoughts (simple sentences) joined by a coordinating conjunction (FANBOYS: for, and, nor, but, or, yet, so) or a semicolon.

> I wanted to go for a walk, but it started raining.

> She likes tea; he prefers coffee.

> Every morning birds chirp outside my window, and my dog barks at them.

COMPLEX SENTENCE

A complex sentence has one complete thought and at least one incomplete thought with a subordinating conjunction (because, although, since, if, when) or a relative pronoun (who, which) connecting them.

> Because I was late (incomplete thought), I missed the meeting (complete thought).

> I'll call you (complete thought) when I arrive (incomplete thought).

COMPOUND-COMPLEX SENTENCE

A compound-complex sentence has at least two complete thoughts and at least one incomplete thought. It combines features of compound and complex sentences.

Examples:

> Although I was tired (incomplete thought), I finished my homework (complete thought), **and** I went to bed (complete thought).

> She didn't come (complete thought) because she was sick (incomplete thought), **but** she sent a message (complete thought).

Let's look at that same passage from the "vary sentence beginnings" section, but now with sentence types not varied.

Original:

> We often turn on ourselves with a defeatist attitude. This happens far more often than you'd expect. Without any warning, this thinking leads us down a rabbit hole. Thus, many of us wind up giving up. Most of us don't have a support system in place at the beginning. This makes it more difficult. You need someone near you to shake you back to your senses.
>
> Luckily, you don't have to suffer through the process. You can tell yourself to keep it simple and operate in a realistic fashion. After this, your success sits within your reach.
>
> *Four sentences no longer start with the subject, but they are all simple sentences.*

Revised:

> We often turn on ourselves with a defeatist attitude, which happens far more often than you'd expect (complex). Without any warning, this thinking leads us down a rabbit hole, and many of us wind up giving up because the experience is too painful (compound-complex). Most of us don't have a support system in

place at the beginning, making it even more difficult. To combat this, you need someone near you to shake you back to your senses.

The great news is that you don't have to suffer through the process. If you can tell yourself to keep it simple and operate in a realistic fashion, success sits within your reach (complex).

This still has the sentence-beginning variety, but now I created a compound-complex sentence and two complex sentences.

Self-editing in practice

Original:

Riley built her business by offering copywriting services to small brands. Clients appreciated her attention to detail and fast turn-around, giving her referrals. These referrals brought in steady work during her first year. New clients came from networking events, local meetups, and even Instagram. She then expanded her offerings to include brand strategy and content planning. Her income doubled by the end of year two.

> ## PAUSE HERE
>
> Open your personalized workbook on your computer and review the practice exercise, asking
>
> - When you read this aloud, does it have a strong, varied rhythm, or does it feel a bit "samey"?
> - Do several sentences start similarly or follow the same basic pattern?
> - Are most of the sentences roughly the same length and type, or do you hear a mix of shorter/longer and different structures?
>
> After answering, revise the passage for better sentence fluency before reading my revision.

Problems with original:

Every sentence is a simple sentence that starts with the subject, and nearly all are the same length.

Revised:

> Focusing on small brands, Riley built a successful copywriting business. She worked hard in her business, and clients appreciated her attention to detail and fast turnaround, giving her referrals. These referrals brought in steady work during her first year. While the referrals were coming in, she made sure to bring in other new clientele by engaging in networking events, local meetups, and even Instagram. She then expanded her offerings to include brand strategy and content planning. Because she constantly worked on and in the business, she doubled her income by the end of year two.

I changed some sentences to begin with other patterns and used simple, compound, and complex sentences. The original contained only simple sentences starting with the subject.

EDITING STEPS

❑ Pause when a section sounds flat, repetitive, or monotonous. (Don't just look at one paragraph. Read multiple paragraphs in the section to detect hidden rhythm issues.)

❑ Check your sentence beginnings: Do too many in a row follow the same beginning pattern even if the first word varies?

❑ Check the sentence lengths and types: Are most of the sentences the same length? Do they follow the same type?

❑ Revise with intentional variety if you answered yes to any of the above questions.

Eliminate Excess "Be" Verbs

William Zinsser said, "Use active verbs unless there is no comfortable way to get around using a passive verb."[10]

"Be" verbs are not active verbs, and newer writers tend to overuse them. (Although let's clear up a common misconception: Using "be" verbs doesn't automatically mean you have passive voice.) "Be" verbs describe state of being:

- Is
- Am
- Are
- Was
- Were
- Be
- Being
- Been

These words are not always bad, but they are weaker than active, powerful verbs. Also, be verbs often cause sentences to be more wordy than needed.

Watch what happens when I rewrite the previous paragraph without "be" verbs: Despite sometimes needing "be" verbs, strong writers revise sentences to use active, powerful verbs. This trims unnecessary words.

(Do you see what I did there? I eliminated the "be" verbs from the section explaining "be" verbs. I know . . . so clever.)

You don't need to eliminate "be" verbs entirely. Just avoid overusing them. Keep the "be" verb if revising around it would change the sentence's

---

10 William Zinsser, *On Writing Well: The Classic Guide to Writing Nonfiction, 30th anniversary ed.* (New York: HarperCollins, 2006), 67.

meaning, weaken the passage, or make the sentence clunky. Total elimination isn't the goal. Improving your writing is.

Methods to reduce "Be" verbs

Use these strategies to reduce "be" verbs when needed.

1. Change the main verb from an –ing to a regular verb. (But be careful: This does change the verb tense from past progressive to simple past, and sometimes you need the progressive tense for vibe, feeling, or accuracy.)

> Original: The moon was rising in the sky.
>
> Revised: The moon rose in the sky.

2. Change the "be" verb to a strong action verb.

> Original: Tony is afraid of notebook checks.
>
> Revised: Tony fears notebook checks.

3. Write one or more showing sentence(s).

> Original: That alligator is aggressive.
>
> Revised: The alligator lurched forward and swallowed the boy's cat.

4. Rearrange the order of the sentence.

> Original: The monster was in the dark tunnel creeping.
>
> Revised: Down the dark tunnel crept the monster.

5. Combine sentences.

> Original: The inefficient time manager is unfulfilled. He heads to bed, disappointed, despite having finished his to-do list.

> Revised: The inefficient time manager heads to bed, unfulfilled, having checked off everything on his to-do list.

6. Change another word to the verb.

> Original: Charles Schulz was the creator of the Peanuts cartoon strip.

> Revised: Charles Schulz created the Peanuts cartoon strip.

7. Get rid of unnecessary phrases

> Original: The fact that he was late to the meeting was why the project didn't start on time.

> Revised: His lateness delayed the project.

Examples

(These all come from books I have edited.)

Original:

> This book **is** a guide to help you manage your stress and systemize your home so you have time for you. It **was** designed for moms who want to help their child but **are** overwhelmed with the demands that come with parenting a special needs child.

Revised:

This guide empowers overwhelmed moms who want to help their special needs child. It provides tools to manage your stress and streamline your home so you have time for *you*.

I combined sentences (method 5) and used a stronger verb—provide (method 2).

Original:

We went about many mornings where he **was** refusing to do it on his own. That **was** the one thing that I **was** working on that morning with him, so I didn't stress about helping him with everything else.

Revised:

While many mornings he refused to do it on his own, I only focused on getting him to put on his socks and didn't stress about everything else.

I changed -ing verb to simple verb (method 1) and got rid of unnecessary phrases—"that was the one thing that I was working on" (method 7).

Original:

"I **was** able to adapt to changing environments." Through shadowing these assistants, I **was** provided insights into the world of work and how the ICT operates in large bodies. [. . .] My placement at this hospital **is** the one thing that helped me the most. I **am** now able to work under pressure and adapt to changing environments.

Revised:

> I found work as a care home administrative assistant, where I learned how to work under pressure and adapt to changing environments. Through shadowing these assistants during my BT placement, I gained insights into the world of work and how ICT operates in large bodies.

I changed the verb to a stronger one—found, gained, and learned (method 2)—and got rid of unnecessary phrases—"is the one thing that helped me" (method 7).

Self-editing in practice

Original:

> My first year as a freelancer was full of challenges. It was a time of uncertainty and learning. I was unsure of how to get clients, and I was constantly worried about money. There were many moments when I was ready to give up. I was told by friends that it would take time, but I wasn't sure how much time I could afford to wait. My confidence was low, and I was overwhelmed by all the advice that was available online. It was difficult to know what path to follow (generated by ChatGPT).

> ## PAUSE HERE
>
> Open your personalized workbook on your computer and review the practice exercise, asking
>
> - How many "be" verbs (is, was, were, am, be, been, being) are in this passage?
> - Do any of those sentences feel vague, static, or wordy because of the "be" verb?
>
> After answering, rewrite to reduce the number of "be" verbs before comparing to mine.

Problem with original:

Original has twelve be verbs, weakening the passage.

Revised:

> In my first year as a freelancer, I faced many challenges. I worried how I would get clients and an income. At times, I wanted to give up, but others told me it would take time and a willingness to learn. That sounded fine and all, but I wasn't sure if I could afford to wait. With low confidence and overwhelmed by all the available advice, I struggled to know what path to follow.

> *Notice I kept "wasn't sure" on purpose. Replacing it with something like "I doubted" or "I questioned" wouldn't have sounded as natural or accurate in this context. The goal isn't elimination; it's improvement, so I chose to leave that one in.*

EDITING STEPS

❑ Stop when a passage feels wordy, flat, or overly dependent on "be" verbs.

❑ Scan the section for an overuse of "be" verbs.

❑ Revise by reducing "be" verbs using any of the six strategies:

- Swap for a stronger verb
- Cut "be" verb and change –ing form of verb
- Show instead of tell
- Change another word in the sentence to the verb
- Combine sentences
- Rearrange sentence order
- Get rid of unnecessary phrases

Reduce Wordiness

We all get wordy sometimes. I'm the wordiness queen—just ask my husband. Even though I struggle to stay concise, I can still edit out wordiness in others' writing. Before we start, let's clarify upfront: Reducing wordiness isn't just about shortening long sentences. Long sentences aren't automatically wordy; they can be powerful when used well. Wordiness often occurs when sentences rely on lots of little or unnecessary words, which also occurs in short sentences.

So don't avoid long sentences; just make sure every word earns its place.

Words and phrases to cut

QUALIFIERS

Words like "really," "quite," "often," etc. aren't always necessary.

Original sentence: I felt really sad.

Revised options: I felt depressed. I felt sad.

PREPOSITIONAL PHRASES

Prepositions show location, time, and place: "of," "under," "from," "above," "at," etc.

You can often replace prepositional phrases with one-word modifiers or reword them to avoid using them.

> Original 18 words: The president **of the student body** decided to combine their homecoming dance **with the one at Neptune High**.

> Revised 10 words: The **student body president** combined homecoming dances **with Neptune High**.

> *The original had three prepositional phrases ("of the student body," "with the one," and "at Neptune High"). The revised only has one ("with Neptune High").*

NOMINALIZATIONS (USING VERBS OR ADJECTIVES AS NOUNS)

These words often end in "-ion," "-ment," "-ity/ty," or "ness." To reduce wordiness, convert nominalizations into verbs.

> Original 9 words: I made the **decision** to write this lesson now.

> Revised 7 words: I **decided** to write this lesson now.

> Original 14 words: It is my **recommendation** that you try each of these habits for one week.

> Revised 9 words: I **recommend** you try each habit for one week.

> *Bonus, I also got rid of an unnecessary prepositional phrase ("of these") and the expletive phrase "it is."*

ADJECTIVIZATIONS (USING VERBS AS ADJECTIVES)

Convert them to verbs.

Original 10 words: Seeing these can clearly be **indicative** of a wordy sentence.

Revised 7 words: Seeing these can **indicate** a wordy sentence.

Original 14 words: I was **successful** in getting my daughter to bed so I could continue writing.

Revised 13 words: I **succeeded** in getting my daughter to bed so I could continue writing.

EXPLETIVE CONSTRUCTIONS

Expletives serve no grammatical function: there are, there is, it is, it was. Sometimes they're the best choice but not always.

Original 8 words: **There were** toys scattered all over the room.

Revised 7 words: Toys were scattered all over the room.

Original 5 words: **It is** fun to write.

Revised 3 words: Writing is fun.

WHICH OR THAT CONSTRUCTIONS

Omit "which" or "that" phrases when possible.

Original 12 words: The cafeteria, **which was new and spacious,** served better food than before.

Revised 9 words: The **new, spacious** cafeteria served better food than before.

Original 12 words: The sheet **that is the most efficient and organized** is my scheduler.

Revised 8 words: The **most efficient, organized sheet** is my scheduler.

Combining sentences to reduce wordiness

Combine sentences when using "this" to refer to the previous sentence.

Original 18 words: My nanny now cleans for one hour. **This has allowed** me to spend more time with my kids.

Revised 16 words: My nanny now cleans for one hour**, allowing** me to spend more time with my kids.

You can also combine sentences by using colons or -ing words or by omitting redundant parts.

REVISED USING COLON

Original 24 words: The swing dance scene has many dance styles. **These styles are** East Coast swing, West Coast swing, Lindy Hop, shag, Charleston, jive, and jitterbug.

Revised 21 words: The swing dance scene has many dance styles**:** East Coast swing, West Coast swing, Lindy Hop, shag, Charleston, jive, and jitterbug.

REVISED USING –ING WORD

Original 14 words: The crowd pushed away in different directions. **There were now** only two people remaining.

Revised 11 words: The crowd pushed away in different directions, **leaving** only two people.

REVISED THROUGH OMISSION

Original 30 words: Many people get confused with taxes. **Typical points of confusion occur** when configuring allowances on their W-4, determining which filing status to use, and knowing how to fill out forms.

Revised 23 words: Many people get confused when configuring allowances on their W-4, determining which filing status to use, and knowing how to fill out forms.

Self-editing in practice

Original:

There is a tendency among new freelancers to really avoid marketing, which is something that can significantly affect their ability to get consistent clients. It is important that they gain an understanding of what methods actually bring in leads. There are a lot of platforms that are available, but it is not necessary to use every one of them. A clear focus on the right strategy is something that can lead to better results over time (generated by ChatGPT).

> ## PAUSE HERE
>
> Open your personalized workbook on your computer and review the practice exercise, asking
>
> - What type of "words and phrases to cut" did you spot in the passage?
> - If you had to cut 25–30 percent of the words in this passage without losing meaning, what would you remove or condense?
>
> After answering, revise the passage to fix wordiness issues before reviewing mine.

Problems with original (word count 76):

The passage uses qualifiers, expletive constructions, nominalizations, prepositional phrases, and a "which" clause.

Revised:

> New freelancers tend to avoid marketing, affecting their ability to get consistent clients. They must understand what methods generate leads. While many platforms exist to help with this, they don't need to use all of them. Instead, focusing on the right strategy will yield better results.

By eliminating qualifiers, expletive constructions, nominalizations, prepositional phrases, and "which" clauses, I decreased the word count to 46, a 39 percent reduction.

EDITING STEPS

- ❑ Stop when a sentence (even short ones) feels like a mouthful and/or has several little words, and revise to avoid
  - qualifiers
  - prepositional phrases
  - nominalizations
  - adjectivizations
  - expletive constructions
  - unnecessary "which" or "that"
- ❑ Combine sentences that use "this" at the beginning of the second sentence.
- ❑ Check for sentence pairs you can combine using a colon and –ing word or by trimming portions.
- ❑ Revise for conciseness without sacrificing meaning, tone, or clarity.

Maintain Consistent Tone

Your book needs one clear tone throughout, but that doesn't mean robotic consistency. Yes, you can have a moment of joking in your book and a moment of serious teaching. I do. The point is to anchor your writing in one tone with a flexible range so any shifts feel intentional rather than jarring.

You don't want to present yourself as mostly authoritative and formal, then suddenly throw in a phrase like "totally chill." Or open with a warm, encouraging introduction and shift into something that sounds overly academic in the main content.

Examples

Example A:

> I know marketing can feel overwhelming. You're not alone in that. It's totally normal to hesitate when putting yourself out there. But don't worry! We'll walk through it step by step so you find it less scary. The next phase requires the implementation of a multi-channel outreach strategy that ensures maximum lead acquisition and retention rates.

The tone starts out conversational and encouraging, using reassuring language, simple phrasing, and first person. Naturally, the reader expects that tone to carry through the rest of the passage. Instead, the writing suddenly shifts into a formal, academic style, complete with jargon in the final sentence.

Example B:

> You're doing great by simply showing up to this chapter. Progress matters more than perfection. However, many writers fail because they don't stay disciplined long enough to see real results.

The generalization "many writers fail" seems mildly critical after the tone started warm and encouraging.

Example C:

> You can absolutely build momentum with small wins. That's how most writers find their flow. Effective workflow optimization requires careful planning and strategic implementation.

The more corporate tone of the last sentence isn't wrong, but it clashes with the relaxed tone in the opening.

How to spot tone issues

I had this problem with my first draft because I pulled material from several sources—student handouts, blog posts, and brand-new sections written just for this book. The student handouts leaned more formal and used third person, while the original content sounded more conversational. I essentially had a "teacher getting down to business" version of myself and a "let's chat about how I can help" version. The voice didn't completely change—I wrote all of it, after all—but the tone shifts still felt jarring.

In order to spot them, I had to ask some questions. You too can ask these questions:

- Does this sentence feel like the same "voice" as the one before it?
- Does this shift sound like a different version of me (professor me, salesy me, emotional me, corporate me)?
- Would this line feel jarring if someone read the chapter aloud?

If the answer is yes, revise for consistency.

Self-editing in practice

Original:

> When launching an online course, you want to begin with a clear understanding of your target audience. This allows you to tailor your content and delivery style to meet the specific needs and learning preferences of your students. Choosing the right platform also plays a key role; you'll want one that offers strong analytics, easy integration, and a seamless user experience.
>
> Now, if you think you can just slap together a few slides and call it a course, think again. No one's going to sit through your boring slideshow unless you make it at least *kind of* engaging. Add some personality, please. We're not in 2004 (generated by ChatGPT).

> ## PAUSE HERE
>
> Open your personalized workbook on your computer and review the practice exercise, asking
>
> - Where do you notice a shift in tone (more casual, more snarky, more formal)?
>
> - If you had to choose one primary tone for this book, which sentences best reflect that tone, and which sentences feel out of character?
>
> After answering, revise the passage to maintain a consistent tone and then check my answer.

Problem with original:

This has two tones: neutral/informative and snarky.

Revised idea #1 to stay consistently neutral and informative:

> When launching an online course, you want to begin with a clear understanding of your target audience. This allows you to tailor your content, examples, and delivery style to meet the specific needs and learning preferences of your students. Choosing the right platform also plays a key role; you'll want one that offers strong analytics, easy integration, and a seamless user experience.
>
> Then, as you develop your course materials, focus on engagement. Slide decks have their use, but don't rely on them as your only tool. Consider incorporating video, interactive quizzes, or real-world case studies to keep your content dynamic and memorable.

Revised idea #2 to stay consistently snarky and conversational:

> Let's get one thing straight: If you're launching an online course, you'd better know who you're talking to. If you skip that part, your content will land like a motivational poster in a dentist's office—generic and slightly painful. Know your audience so you can actually speak their language.
>
> Also, don't just pick some free, janky platform your cousin Todd used once. You want solid analytics and an interface that won't make your students rage-click out of the lesson.
>
> And please, don't toss together a PowerPoint from 2009 and call it a day. This is your course. Bring the energy. Add stories, humor, something human. Because if you're not into it, why should anyone else be?

EDITING STEPS

- ❏ Review your intro and make sure it sets the tone you want to use throughout the book. If it does, note that tone.
- ❏ Read each chapter and check for mismatches in tone.
- ❏ Look for sections where the language becomes more formal, casual, academic, or emotional than the rest. Highlight any tone shifts that don't match the intended voice. Then revise accordingly.

Ensure Accurate Reading Level

Are you writing to impress your college professors, or to help readers understand and apply your ideas? The answer feels obvious. Still, some authors try to sound impressive. When sentences grow too complex or vocabulary starts to show off, your readers struggle to absorb the message, even when the content itself shines. On the other hand, if you oversimplify for a sophisticated audience, that can come across as condescending.[11]

Most general nonfiction aimed at a broad audience should target a seventh- to ninth-grade reading level. This speaks to readability, not to the ideas themselves. Your ideas can be complex and geared to adults; just express them clearly. With that said, audience matters here too. With a highly specific group, your ideal reading level may need to fall below or above the general range.

Determine your reading level

Use Microsoft Word's built-in readability checker:

1. Go to File →Options → Proofing
2. Check "Show readability statistics"
3. Run spell check (Review → Spelling & Grammar)
4. After spell check completes, a box will display your Flesch-Kincaid Grade Level and Flesch Reading Ease score

---

11 Portions of this topic were drafted with AI assistance, then I edited and reviewed the output.

Flesch-Kincaid Grade Level: Shows what grade level is needed to understand your text

- 8.0: eighth-grade level
- 12.0: twelfth grade/high school senior level
- 16.0: college level

Flesch Reading Ease: Scores text on a 100-point scale (higher = easier)

- 90–100: Very easy (fifth grade)
- 60—70: Standard (eighth to ninth grade)
- 30–50: Difficult (college level)
- 0–30: Very difficult (graduate level)

What affects reading level

Several factors influence readability scores:

- Sentence length: Shorter sentences are easier to process[12]
- Word length: Simpler words (fewer syllables) increase readability
- Paragraph length: Dense paragraphs feel harder to read than shorter ones
- Passive voice: Active voice is generally clearer and more direct
- Technical jargon: Specialized terms increase reading difficulty

Adjusting reading level

If your score is too high:

- Break long sentences into shorter ones
- Replace complex words with simpler alternatives where possible (use "help" instead of "facilitate")
- Cut unnecessary words and phrases
- Use active voice instead of passive voice

---

12 As mentioned in the vary sentences lesson, long sentences aren't bad in and of themselves. Too many does increase your reading level score.

If your score is too low and feels overly simplistic:

You probably don't need to adjust because clear writing nearly always serves readers better. If your audience works in a highly specialized field (academic, technical), then use more complex sentence structures and industry-specific terminology.

But don't obsess over hitting an exact number. Readability scores offer helpful guidance, not absolute rules. Some concepts require complex sentences, and that's okay. A chapter on neuroscience will naturally score higher than a chapter on time management tips.

Self-editing in practice

Original passage (Flesch-Kincaid Grade Level: 12.3):

The implementation of effective time management strategies necessitates a comprehensive understanding of one's cognitive limitations and behavioral patterns. Individuals who fail to acknowledge the finite nature of their attentional resources frequently overcommit to professional obligations, consequently experiencing diminished productivity and heightened psychological stress. Furthermore, the utilization of digital task management systems, while potentially beneficial, often exacerbates the problem by facilitating an unrealistic accumulation of commitments. To optimize temporal allocation, one must systematically evaluate competing priorities through a methodical assessment of their alignment with overarching objectives, subsequently declining opportunities that fail to contribute meaningfully to strategic goals (generated by Claude).

> ## PAUSE HERE
>
> Open your personalized workbook on your computer and review the practice exercise, asking
>
> - Which words or phrases feel overly formal, academic, or abstract for a general nonfiction reader?
> - Where do long sentences or dense wording make the ideas harder to grasp on a first read?
> - How could you say the same thing using simpler words, shorter sentences, or more direct "you" language without dumbing it down?
>
> After answering, revise the passage to make it easier to understand, then check my answer.

Problems with original:

This contains too many long sentences (each one is twenty-five words or more), complex vocabulary (necessitates, exacerbates, temporal allocation), formal/academic tone, and abstract phrasing.

Revised (to a Flesch-Kincaid Grade Level of 7.8):

> Effective time management requires you to understand your limits. You can't focus on everything, and when you overcommit, your productivity drops while your stress rises. Digital task management apps can help, but they also make it easy to add too many tasks to your list.
>
> To get more done in less time, you must review your priorities. Ask which tasks align with your main goals. Then decline opportunities that don't support those goals.

Revision tactics:

- Replaced complex words with simpler alternatives (necessitates → requires, temporal allocation → get more done in less time)
- Broke long sentences into shorter ones (original had a forty-word sentence)
- Cut wordy phrases (fail to contribute meaningfully → don't support)

EDITING STEPS

❑ Run a readability check on a few sample chapters to establish your baseline reading level.

❑ Compare your score to your target audience's needs (seventh to ninth grade for general nonfiction, higher for specialized audiences).

❑ If your score is too high, identify sections with:
- Long sentences (20+ words)
- Complex vocabulary
- Passive voice
- Abstract or formal phrasing

❑ Revise using these strategies:
- Break long sentences into shorter ones
- Replace complex words with simpler alternatives
- Convert passive voice to active voice
- Use concrete examples instead of abstract concepts
- Speak directly to the reader using "you"

❑ Run another readability check on the revised sections to ensure improvement.

STOP: DON'T READ AHEAD YET

Apply the two or three topics you chose for this pass to your manuscript before moving on.

This book is a toolbox, not a linear book. You'll get the most value from doing the work as you go.

If you haven't done so yet, scan the QR code or visit https://beaconpointservices.org/nonfiction-editing -workbook to generate your personalized workbook for the writing pass.

When you're ready, come back and begin the next pass.

You've got this.

TECHNICAL PASS

Grammar, spelling, capitalization, and punctuation . . . oh my! Yep, you're stepping back into English class for a minute. Sorry, well, actually not really. If you're going to be a writer, you need to know the basics. If you were in my actual class, we'd have so much fun with this: jokes galore, maybe even some rapping or tap dancing, or even an interpretive dance about commas. But you're not in my actual classroom. You're reading a book. So I'll spare you the tap shoes and focus on what matters most: the small tweaks that will make the biggest difference.

During this pass focus on fixing actual errors, the grammar, spelling, capitalization, and punctuation mistakes that distract readers. Since comprehensive coverage of all the rules would make this guide overwhelming, I've focused on the most common errors I see in each category (spelling, punctuation, capitalization, and grammar). I also included a topic on source attribution because it's essential for credibility.

Start by doing the general find-and-replace tasks (they're quick wins). Then pick just two to three topics to read and apply in this pass, focusing on the ones your book needs most. Of course, you'll want to fix any errors you catch, but to start, just focus on the topics you chose.

Remember, I'm also developing a manuscript diagnostic tool designed to help authors pinpoint their highest-priority editing topics more quickly and accurately, using an editorial eye rather than an author's eye. In the meantime, I offer Manuscript Checkup services that provide personalized guidance to help you decide what to self-edit for. See appendix A to learn about both options.

Make sure to do the find-and-replace tasks (starts on page 138), then pick two or three topics from these options:

- Correct easily confused words (page 144)
- Fix common comma errors (page 155)
- Correct unnecessary capitalization (page 164)
- Revise misplaced modifiers (page 169)
- Verify source attributions (page 177)

Personalized workbook: To generate your customizable technical pass workbook, scan the QR code or visit https://beaconpointservices. org/nonfiction-editing-workbook.

For best results, open on a computer or tablet to download and edit the Word document.

Run General Find-and-Replace Checks

The easiest fixes take five minutes and a few clicks—if you know what to look for. They're just simple find-and-replace tasks. An editor can easily fix them too, but why leave it to them when you can easily just do the thing yourself?

The next few steps are quick Word tricks (I promise), and once you know them, you'll fly through cleanup. This lesson differs from the rest because it doesn't include an editing practice or editing steps. The editing steps are simply to perform the find-and-replace tasks outlined below.

> **Software**
>
> While the screenshots and examples come from Word on a PC, all major word-processing programs have a find-and-replace feature.

To use find and replace, go to Find on the Word ribbon and select "Advanced Find."

This brings up a box with "Find what" and "Replace with." In the instructions below, anything in parentheses represents a button you press, not text you actually type. So (space) would indicate you press the space bar, not type in "space."

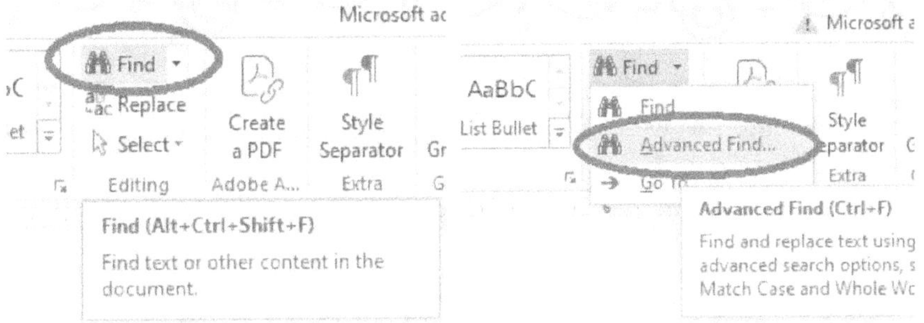

Eliminate double spaces after periods

Find what: (space)(space)

Replace with: (space)

You may have been taught to insert two spaces after a period. I was taught this way, too, and I did struggle to break the habit at first. Back when typewriters were a thing, double spaces were necessary. Now, they aren't. So eliminating them is an easy win.

Tabbed indents

Find what: ^t

Replace with: [leave this blank]

Paragraphs shouldn't be indented by pressing "tab." When your book gets to the design stage, these indents won't transfer. Editors use Word Styles to get your paragraphs to indent automatically. Don't worry about Word Styles right now, but do get rid of any tabbed indents. If you want to include indents in your document without using Word Styles (your editor will apply those), then do the following:

Highlight your entire document by hitting Ctrl + A. Then, in the Paragraph section of the toolbar, click on the arrow in the right-hand corner. Or right-click (PC) or triple-click (Mac) to open the paragraph pop-up window.

A dialogue box will pop up. Under "Special," select "First line." Under "By," select "0.5" (or whatever you want the indent to be, but this is the standard). Then click OK.

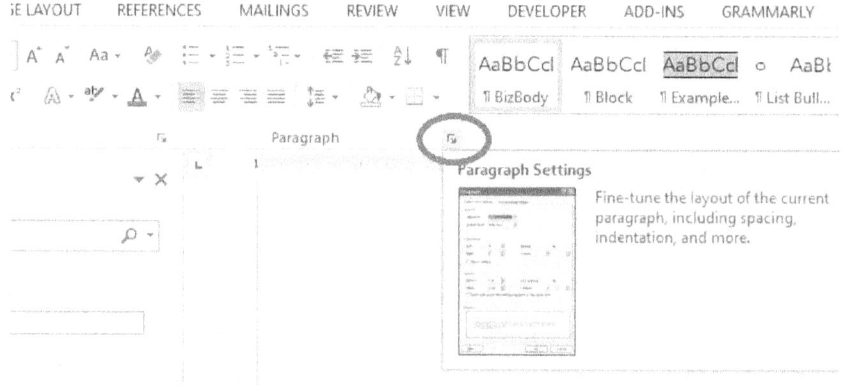

Straight quotes

First, make sure your document is set up to autocorrect straight quotes to smart quotes. This is the default setting, so it's most likely already the case. But just in case, go to File → Options → Proofing. Then click on the "Autocorrect Options" button. From there, select "Autoformat" and make sure "Change straight quotes to smart quotes" is selected. Then, in the find-and-replace box, enter straight, not curly, quotation marks.

For single quotes:

Find: '

Replace: '

For double quotes:

Find: "

Replace: "

Yes, you're typing the exact same thing in the find-and-replace box, but since it's set to autocorrect to curly (smart) quotes, it'll put in the correct ones.

Eliminate soft returns

Unless you intentionally put in a soft return (a manual line break), remove all soft returns. If you don't know what a soft return is, you most likely didn't use them on purpose.

Find what: ^l [that's a lowercase L]

Replace with: ^p [that's a paragraph break]

Change double returns to single

This will remove unnecessary spaces between paragraphs. You never want double returns in your document.

Find what: ^p^p

Replace with: ^p

Em and en dashes

If you're following the Chicago Manual of Style (CMoS), use em dashes, not en dashes, to surround parenthetical elements. If you're following

British style, use en dashes. CMoS recommends unspaced em dashes, but if you prefer to space them out, that's fine. Just let your editor know.

Example	How to change to this from unspaced hyphens	How to change to this from spaced hyphens	How to change to this from spaced en dash
Unspaced em dash My son—the cutest kid ever—has learned how to army crawl.	Find: – Replace: ^+	Find: (space)–(space) Replace: ^+	Find: (space)^=(space) Replace: ^+
Spaced em dash My son — the cutest kid ever — has learned to army crawl.	Find: – Replace: (space)^+(space)	Find: (space)–(space) Replace: (space)^+(space)	Find: (space)^=(space) Replace: (space)^+(space)
Spaced en dash My son – the cutest kid ever – has learned to army crawl.	Find: – Replace: (space)^=(space)	Find: (space)–(space) Replace: (space)^=(space)	

Change hyphen between numbers to an en dash

With a range of numbers, use an en dash rather than a hyphen. So it should be 3–20, not 3-20.

Make sure you check the "Use wildcards" box, or this find and replace won't work. To enable wildcards, click on "More" and select "Use wildcards."

Find: ([0-9+])-([0-9+])

Replace: \1^=\2

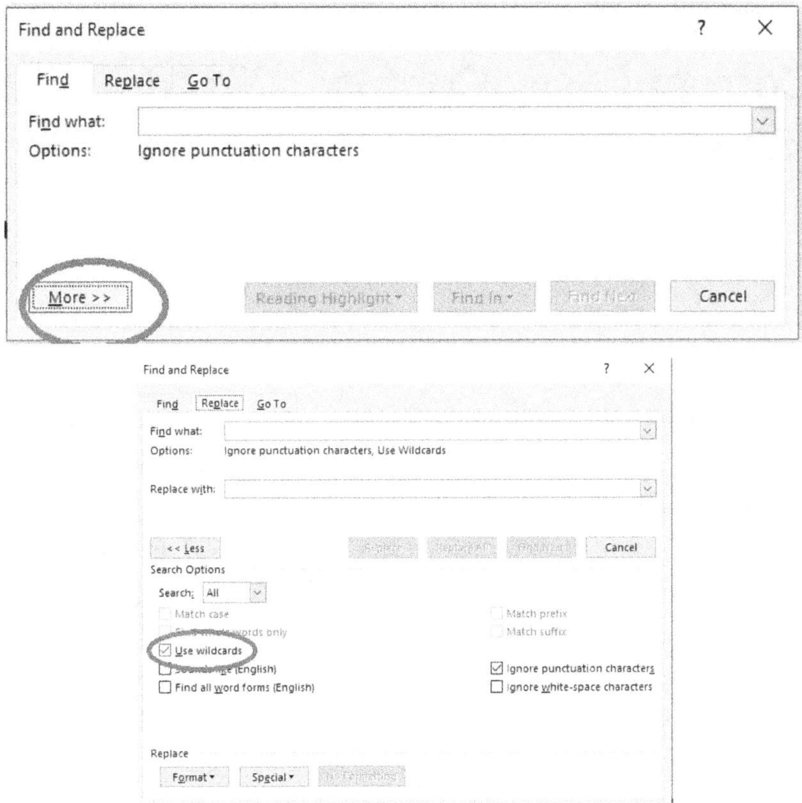

Once you run these quick fixes, your manuscript will be cleaner. Yay for easy wins!

Correct Easily Confused Words (Spelling)

I have a mortifying confession: I'm a professional editor, and I still mix up "lose" and "loose." I know the difference. I even teach the difference. But my fingers don't always cooperate with my brain.

Do you know your troublesome words too (to)? It's easier than (then?) you think to find and fix them. You're (your?) just going to use some research skills and Word's Find feature.

These little errors don't make you a bad writer. They just make your writing look less polished, and readers tend to assign credibility based on technical accuracy.

So let's walk through the most common offenders.

Please note, this isn't an all-inclusive list. I recommend Debbie Emmitt's Tricky Quickies series to learn more (see appendix B for the link to this and other resources).

Your/You're

Your = possessive → something belongs to you
You're = you are

Examples:

> Your example was excellent.
> You're doing a great job self-editing.

Quick tip: If you can replace the word with "you are," use "you're."

Their/There/They're

Their = possessive

There = location or a dummy subject ("There's . . .")

They're = they are

Examples:

> The team shared their results.
>
> Put the report over there.
>
> They're presenting tomorrow.

Quick tip: "They're" must always expand to "they are."

It's/Its

It's = it is

Its = possessive (yes, English likes chaos)

Examples:

> It's a great idea.
>
> The system updated its settings.

Quick tip: If you can't expand to "it is," you need "its."

Accept/Except

Accept = to receive or agree to

Except = excluding

Examples:

I cannot accept that edit.

Everyone attended except Jonathan.

Quick tip: If you can replace it with "receive," it's "accept."

Good/Well

Good = adjective → describes nouns
Well = adverb → describes actions

Examples

She wrote a good proposal.

She writes well.

Quick tip: If it describes *how someone does something* → "well."

Into/In to

Into = movement/transformation
In to = the word in followed by to

Examples

She walked into the room.

I logged in to update the file.

Quick tip: If you can swap the word with "inside," use "into."

Chose/Choose

Chose = past tense

Choose = present/future

Examples:

> Yesterday, I chose a topic.

> Today, I'll choose headings.

Lose/Loose

Lose = to misplace or be deprived of

Loose = not tight

Examples:

> I don't want to lose momentum.

> These pants are too loose.

Quick tip: Double O in "loose" → extra space → not tight.

Affect/Effect

Affect = verb, to influence

Effect = noun, a result

Examples:

> That comment didn't affect my edits.

> The effect was improved clarity.

Quick tip: "Affect" = action (both start with A). "Effect" = end result (both start with E).

Sell/Sale

Sell = verb
Sale = noun

Examples:

> I sell editing services.
>
> The book is on sale.

Quick tip: If you can put "a" or "the" before it, use "sale."

Principal/Principle

Principal = noun, main person in charge of a school; adjective, most important
Principle = rule, value, or concept

Examples:

> Our principal concern is clarity.
>
> It's a matter of principle.

Quick tip: Principal = PAL (your principal is your pal).

Advice/Advise

Advice = noun
Advise = verb

Examples:

> Thank you for the advice.
>
> I advise running a read-aloud pass.

Illicit/Elicit

Illicit = illegal

Elicit = to draw out

Examples:

> That was an illicit document leak.
>
> The story will elicit emotion.

Further/Farther

Further = metaphorical distance

Farther = physical distance

Examples:

> Let's take this idea further.
>
> She walked three miles farther.

Lay/Lie/Laid

Lay = present tense of "to lay" (requires an object)

Lay = past tense of "to lie" (no object)

Lie = to recline

Laid = past tense of lay

Examples:

> I lay the book down.
>
> I want to lie down.
>
> I laid my keys by the door so I wouldn't forget them.
>
> Yesterday I lay on the couch for an hour.

(This one consistently hurts people's souls. It's okay.)

Then/Than

Then = time

Than = comparison

Examples:

> First we draft, then we revise.

> Editing takes longer than most people expect.

Whether/Weather

Whether = choice

Weather = rain/sun/snow

Examples:

> I'm deciding whether this chapter needs another example.

> I love living in Utah but hate the weather.

Fewer/Less

Fewer = countable items

Less = mass quantity or uncountable concepts

Examples:

> This chapter has fewer examples than the last one.

> The new outline requires less work overall.

Complement/Compliment

Complement = completes

Compliment = praise

Examples:

> Your introduction complements the chapter beautifully.
>
> He complimented me on the structure of the final draft.

Self-editing in practice

These practices offer separate paragraphs rather than one cohesive example, giving you individual passages to work on misspelled words.

Original A:

> I tried to accept all the feedback gracefully, except for the comment about my tone—that one still bothers me. I'm not sure how much it will effect my final draft, but I hope it doesn't affect my confidence too much.
>
> Yesterday, I lay the folders on the table and asked my assistant to lay them out neatly while I went to lay down. Instead, she just lay them in a messy pile and left early.
>
> Your welcome to take over that part of the project if you're up for a challenge. Their probably not going to finish on time, and there already behind schedule.
>
> The principal reason we choose that vendor was reliability, but now I wonder if we should have chosen someone else. It's a matter of principle at this point.

> **PAUSE HERE**
>
> Open your personalized workbook on your computer and correct the misspelled words, then check my revision for the answers.

Revised A:

I tried to accept all the feedback gracefully, except for the comment about my tone—that one still bothers me. I'm not sure how much it will **affect** my final draft, but I hope it doesn't affect my confidence too much.

Yesterday, I **laid** the folders on the table and asked my assistant to lay them out neatly while I went to **lie** down. Instead, she just **laid** them in a messy pile and left early.

You're welcome to take over that part of the project if you're up for a challenge. **They're** probably not going to finish on time, and **they're** already behind schedule.

The principal reason we **chose** that vendor was reliability, but now I wonder if we should have chosen someone else. It's a matter of principle at this point.

Original B:

She wanted to advise him on the best course of action, but he didn't seem to want the advice. He was more focused on the effect the decision would have on their team's morale rather than the affect it might have on profits.

He glanced at the display and said, "Wow, that's a great sale on monitors." But I had to tell him that the sign actually said they wouldn't be on sell until next week. So I couldn't sale it to him today at that price. I told him to come back tomorrow, but he chose not to except that and got really mad.

He ran half a mile further than anyone else on the team, hoping to further impress the coach. He had less natural talent than the others, but he knew he made up for that in determination. He just needed less people distracting him, mainly his girlfriend.

PAUSE HERE

Open your personalized workbook on your computer and correct the misspelled words, then check my revision for the answers.

Revised B:

She wanted to advise him on the best course of action, but he didn't seem to want the advice. He was more focused on the effect the decision would have on their team's morale rather than the **effect** it might have on profits.

He glanced at the display and said, "Wow, that's a great sale on monitors." But I had to tell him that the sign actually said they wouldn't be on **sale** until next week. So I couldn't **sell** it to him today at that price. I told him to come back tomorrow, but he chose not to **accept** that and got really mad.

He ran half a mile **farther** than anyone else on the team, hoping to further impress the coach. He had less natural talent than the others, but he knew he made up for that in determination. He just needed **fewer** people distracting him, mainly his girlfriend.

EDITING STEPS

❏ Use Word's Find feature to search for the first word in a pair you tend to confuse.

❏ For each result, check whether the word is used correctly in context.

❏ Search for the second word in the pair and review its usage.

❏ Repeat with each word pair you struggle with.

Fix Common Comma Errors (Punctuation)

Commas are a pain, and I say that as an editor. We editors constantly ask each other comma questions, and we debate what's correct more often than you'd think. So if even professional editors can't always agree on commas, you shouldn't feel discouraged when you struggle with them!

But here's the good news: Despite dozens of comma rules, most manuscripts see the same four errors over and over: comma splice, run-on, introductory error, and fused sentence. Master these four, and you'll catch the majority of your comma problems.

Commas with coordinating conjunctions (comma splices and run-ons)

Let's call these conjunctions FANBOYS: <u>f</u>or, <u>a</u>nd, <u>n</u>or, <u>b</u>ut, <u>o</u>r, <u>y</u>et, <u>s</u>o. These words join parts of sentences and have clear rules for when you need a comma.

Rule 1. When a FANBOYS word joins phrases, skip the comma—though you may choose to add one for stylistic reasons.

Rule 2. When a FANBOYS word joins independent clauses, include the comma. You can't have just a comma between two sentences, nor can you rely on just the FANBOYS. You need both.

Clause example:

> My daughter loves "riding" her bike, but she really is just walking her bike around the kitchen.

> *Both clauses could be sentences by themselves. My daughter loves "riding" her bike. She really is just walking her bike around the kitchen. So, since a FANBOYS is joining them, you need that comma before "but."*

Phrase example:

> My daughter loves "riding" her bike but doesn't do it right.

> *"Doesn't do it right" functions as a phrase since it lacks a subject, so no comma is required before the "but."*

Error 1. Comma splice (comma but no FANBOYS):

> I love punctuation marks, they are fun to play with.

Fix options:

> I love punctuation marks**.** They are fun to play with.

> I love punctuation marks**, for** they are fun to play with.

Error 2. Run-on (FANBOYS but no comma):

> I love punctuation marks but the em dash and colon are my favorites.

Fix:

> I love punctuation marks, but the em dash and colon are my favorites.

Fused sentences

You have three ways to join two or more independent clauses. Of course, you can just use a period and create separate sentences. But if you opt to join the clauses, use one of these three methods: Both a comma and a FANBOYS, a semicolon, or, in certain situations, a colon. But with no punctuation between two independent clauses, you have a fused sentence.

> Fused sentence: I love playing basketball it is fun.
>
> Correct: I love playing basketball**, for** it is fun.
>
> Correct: I love playing basketball; it is fun.

Commas with introductions

A comma usually goes after sentence introductions (a word, clause, or phrase that comes before the independent clause).

SINGLE-WORD

One word that modifies the meaning of an entire clause.

> Surprisingly, the roof was still intact.
>
> *You need a comma after your one-word sentence intro-duction.*

The exception to this is when the one-word sentence introduction indicates when something happened.

Often I snack in the afternoon.

No comma needed after "often."

SUBORDINATING CLAUSE

Subordinating clauses begin with a subordinating conjunction (after, although, as, when, while, until, unless, before, because, if, since) and don't express a complete thought.

If they want to do well on the test, students must spend time studying.

"If they want to do well on the test" contains a subject (they) and verb (want), but it doesn't express a complete thought. It begins with a subordinating conjunction (if). Comma goes at the end of the dependent clause and before the main clause: Students must spend time studying.

INFINITIVE PHRASE

Begins with the infinitive form of a verb (to + base verb)

To stay in shape for competition, athletes must exercise every day.

Begins with to + verb (stay) and doesn't contain a subject. Comma goes at the end of the entire infinitive phrase and before the main clause: Athletes must exercise every day.

> **Tip**
>
> Watch out for sentences where the infinitive phrase functions as the subject of the sentence: To start a new business without doing market research and long-term planning in advance would be foolish. (No comma between "advance" and "would" because it doesn't function as an introductory phrase—it acts as the subject of the sentence.)

PARTICIPIAL PHRASE

A participial phrase begins with a past or present participle (–ed or –ing form of a verb that functions as an adjective).

Throwing caution to the wind, she told him she loved him.

Begins with a present participle (throwing). Comma goes at the end of the entire participial phrase and before the main clause: she told him she loved him.

> **Tip**
>
> Don't confuse a participle with a gerund (an –ing verb functioning as a noun): Singing and dancing at the same time is hard to do. (No comma here because *singing* and *dancing* function as nouns, not adjectives, and serve as the sentence's subject.)

PREPOSITIONAL PHRASE

A prepositional phrase begins with a preposition, a word that indicates position (about, above, across, after, over, under, near, etc.).

Over the Christmas holiday, I cleaned out my attic.

Begins with a preposition (over). Comma goes at the end of the preposi-tional phrase and before the main clause: I cleaned out my attic.

No comma needed after a short prepositional phrase (two to three words), though you can add one for stylistic purposes.

ABSOLUTE PHRASE

An absolute phrase has a noun and modifiers; it also often includes a participle, but not always.

Their tummies satisfied, they crawled into bed.

Their tummies (noun) satisfied (participle). Comma goes at the end of the entire absolute phrase and before the main clause: They crawled into bed.

Self-editing in practice

Original:

My editor said punctuation would be an easy fix I didn't believe her. I thought I had a good handle on commas, but apparently I overuse them, underuse them, and misuse them all at once. It's honestly impressive, I guess. She first flagged my comma splices, those are when you join two full sentences with just a comma.

Then we got to FANBOYS, she said something about clauses and coordinating conjunctions I kinda zoned out. It made more sense when she showed me an example. I had written, "I love edit-ing books, but sometimes I question all my life choices." That one passed. But I also wrote, "Editing takes time but it's always worth it." Apparently that one needed a comma. I can't always tell the difference between a clause and a phrase and that's part of the problem.

When it comes to intros I guess I forget the comma. For example I write things like "To get better I started reading grammar guides." According to my editor I need a comma after those intro bits but not always. It depends on the length.

Participles confused me the most. Throwing grammar rules to the wind I added commas wherever I felt like it. Not a great strategy, it turns out. Over the weekend I rewrote five chapters my brain fried by the end of it. But I'm learning. Slowly.

PAUSE HERE

Open your personalized workbook and correct the common comma errors, then read my revision.

Revised (Note that many comma errors can be fixed in multiple ways. So your fix may be different than mine.):

My editor said punctuation would be an easy fix. I didn't believe her. I thought I had a good handle on commas, but apparently, I overuse them, underuse them, and misuse them all at once. It's honestly impressive, I guess. She first flagged my comma splices: those are when you join two full sentences with just a comma.

Then we got to FANBOYS, **and** she said something about clauses and coordinating conjunctions. I kinda zoned out. It made more sense when she showed me an example. I had written, "I love editing books, but sometimes I question all my life choices." That one passed. But I also wrote, "Editing takes time, but it's always worth it." Apparently, that one needed a comma. I can't always tell the difference between a clause and a phrase, and that's part of the problem.

When it comes to intros, I guess I forget the comma. For example, I write things like "To get better, I started reading grammar guides." According to my editor, I need a comma after those intro bits but not always. It depends on the length.

Participles confused me the most. Throwing grammar rules to the wind, I added commas wherever I felt like it. Not a great strategy, it turns out. Over the weekend I rewrote five chapters, **and** my brain fried by the end of it. But I'm learning. Slowly.

You can opt to put in a comma after "over the weekend." However, short introductions that indicate when something happened do not have to have a comma.

EDITING STEPS

❑ Watch out for run-ons. Check all coordinating conjunctions (FANBOYS) between two clauses. If each side could stand alone as its own sentence, insert a comma before the FANBOYS. If one side is a phrase (not a complete sentence), a comma usually isn't needed, though you can stylistically choose to have one.

❑ Watch out for comma splices. If two sentences are joined with just a comma, fix it by adding the missing FANBOYS or make it a period.

❑ Watch out for fused sentences. If two sentences aren't joined by anything, fix it by using one of the correct methods (comma and FANBOYS, semicolon, colon) or split it into two sentences with a period.

❑ Look at sentences with introductory words, clauses, or phrases. If a sentence starts with something before the main subject-verb clause, check if it needs a comma.

❑ Check that commas enhance clarity, not clutter the sentence. If you're using a comma "just in case," double-check the rule to see if it's actually needed.

Correct Unnecessary Capitalization (Capitalization)

Some writers sprinkle capital letters around like salt. (This analogy works best if you're like my husband and me who put salt on everything.) I get it. Capital letters feel important, like a way to tell the reader, "Hey, look at this part!" But most of the time, unnecessary capitalization just makes your writing look chaotic and amateurish.

I can't teach every capitalization rule here, but the core guideline is simple: capitalize proper nouns. That's it—not important-sounding words or roles or concepts. If it's not a recognized proper noun, don't capitalize it.

What you should capitalize:

- Names of people
- Official book, program, law, policy, or course titles
    - Accounting Issues for Lawyers (but lowercase any reference that doesn't use the full course title, such as "All lawyers should take an accounting class")
    - *The 7 Habits of Highly Effective People*
    - Blue Ribbon Commission on Diversity
    - Federal Privacy Act of 1974, Section 7
- Official framework or system names
    - Myers-Briggs Type Indicator
    - McKinsey 7S model
    - Windows, Chrome

- ○ Scaled Agile Framework
- Job titles *only* when used *before* a person's name
  - ○ President George W. Bush
  - ○ Editor Katie Chambers
- Departments or units with official names
  - ○ the Department of Aerospace Engineering Sciences
  - ○ the College of Arts and Sciences (but lowercase when not the official name, such as "the arts and sciences departments")
- Geographical regions
  - ○ The Rocky Mountain region
  - ○ The Midwest
  - ○ Southern accent
  - ○ Lowercase when a compass direction: The store is farther east

What you should not capitalize:

- Job titles that don't come before a name or are used generically
  - ○ I need to report to the vice principal
  - ○ The president is the most important . . .
  - ○ My book is with my editor
- Concepts
  - ○ vision statement
  - ○ marketing plan
- Steps that aren't officially branded
  - ○ Step one is the content pass, then you go to the organization pass
- Ideas you think are very important
- Words you want to emphasize
- Nouns that "feel special"

Incorrect examples

You need to improve your Mindset so you can reach your Goals.

Mindset and goals may be important concepts in your book, but they're not actual proper nouns.

I had a meeting with the Vice President of the board.

Remember, don't capitalize job titles unless used with a name.

The first step in the Five Pillars of Productivity . . .

You'll create your Marketing Plan in this chapter.

Unless your concept, step, framework, or method has been officially published, no one considers it a proper noun.

Now, you're the author and get the final say (especially if you're self-publishing), so if you truly want certain framework steps capitalized, let your editor know. You're allowed some creative license, but if you overdo it, the excess capitalization can reflect poorly on you.

Self-editing in practice

Original:

Building a consistent Morning Routine doesn't mean you need to force yourself into a rigid system. You just need to choose habits that support your body, your mind, and your long-term Wellness Goals. The biggest theme of the Build a Better You Summit was to Start Small. Maybe drink a glass of water, stretch for five minutes, or review your intention for the day. None of these steps is complicated, but they create momentum. Over time, you'll build what I call your Personal Baseline, the combination of daily choices that help you feel grounded and focused. If you've ever read *Atomic Habits* by James Clear, you know how powerful small steps can be. And no, your Personal Baseline doesn't have to match anyone else's. What matters is identifying the Actions that help you function at your best, and letting go of the ones that drain your energy. I learned this myself after working at the Phoenix Office of the American Heart Association, where stress and burnout were practically part of the dress code (generated by ChatGPT).

PAUSE HERE

Open your personalized workbook and lowercase what shouldn't be capitalized, then check the answers below.

Revised:

Building a consistent **morning routine** doesn't mean you need to force yourself into a rigid system. You just need to choose habits that support your body, your mind, and your long-term **wellness goals**. The biggest theme of the Build a Better You Summit was to **start small**. Maybe drink a glass of water, stretch for five minutes, or review your intention for the day. None of these steps is complicated, but they create momentum. Over time, you'll build what I call your **personal baseline**, the combination of daily choices that help you feel grounded and focused. If you've ever read *Atomic Habits* by James Clear, you know how powerful small steps can be. And no, your personal baseline doesn't have to match anyone else's. What matters is identifying the **actions** that help you function at your best, and letting go of the ones that drain your energy. I learned this myself after working at the Phoenix **o**ffice of the American Heart Association, where stress and burnout were practically part of the dress code.

Kept the proper nouns—name of summit, title of book, author name, official name of an organization, a city—capitalized, but then lowercased everything else.

EDITING STEPS

❑ Check all capitalized words and change them to lowercase if
  - you capitalized them because they "felt important"
  - it's a job title that doesn't come before a name
  - it's a concept, framework, or step that isn't an official name
  - you're using caps for emphasis

❑ If you feel strongly about any of them, let your editor know because they will lowercase them otherwise.

Revise Misplaced Modifiers (Grammar)

Misplaced modifiers are like putting the wrong caption on a photo. The details show up, but they're attached to the wrong subject, creating confusion or unintentional comedy. My husband will show me these reels or memes, and I get confused when the image or video doesn't match the text, usually resulting in him getting annoyed that I'm missing the point. But I end up completely discombobulated. While I enjoy saying the word, it's not a fun state to be in. Don't leave your reader discombobulated; keep your modifiers in the right place.

A modifier is a word or phrase that describes something in your sentence.

Sentence	Modifier	Subject
The meticulous editor carefully reviewed the manuscript.	meticulous (adjective)	editor
The author quickly responded to the editor's feedback.	quickly (adverb)	author
The manuscript on the desk belongs to the client.	on the desk (prepositional phrase)	manuscript
She paused to clarify the sentence structure.	to clarify the sentence structure (infinitive phrase)	she

Sentence	Modifier	Subject
The course, a comprehensive guide to freelancing, is launching next month.	a comprehensive guide to freelancing (appositive)	course
The book that she edited became a bestseller.	that she edited (relative clause)	book

A misplaced modifier happens when the modifier is too far from the subject it's describing, creating confusion (or sometimes unintentional comedy)

Examples

Original A:

The suspects were interviewed right after the crime was committed by the detectives.

"By the detectives" modifies "interviewed," not "committed," so you need to move the modifier.

Revised A:

The suspects were interviewed by the detectives right after the crime was committed.

Or for active voice: The detectives interviewed the suspects . . .

Original B:

While only six years old, members of the board agreed it was time to update the plan.

"Only six years old" modifies "plan," not "members," so you need to move the modifier.

Revised B:

> Members of the board agreed it was time to update the six-year-old plan.

Some misplaced modifiers seem obvious and even funny. Others are harder to spot because the sentence makes sense at first glance.

Tricky instance:

> Dr. Smith sent the report to Dr. Johnson before he left to go on vacation.

The placement of the modifier suggests that Dr. Johnson is going on vacation, even though other clues in the sentence make it clear that Dr. Smith is going. However, that doesn't matter. The modifier is in the wrong place regardless of whether the meaning is clear.

Revised:

> Before he left to go on vacation, Dr. Smith sent the report to Dr. Johnson.

Misplaced adverbs

Single-word adverbs are often misplaced because they have specific rules about whether they come before or after the verb they describe.

Adverbs come in two types:

- Adverbs of manner: describe how an action or event is done
- Adverbs of frequency: describe how often an action or event is done

Where you place the adverb depends on the type of adverb and the structure of the sentence.

ADVERBS OF FREQUENCY

With adverbs of frequency, the adverb comes before the main verb in most cases.

Correct: I **sometimes** <u>forget</u> to lock the door.

Incorrect: I <u>forget</u> **sometimes** to lock the door.

If the verb is a form of "to be," then you place the adverb of frequency after.

Correct: He <u>is</u> **usually** more excited.

Incorrect: He **usually** <u>is</u> more excited.

If the sentence has auxiliary verbs like "do/does" and "have/has," then you should place it between the auxiliary and the main verb.

Correct: He <u>has</u> **never** <u>been</u> out of the country.

Incorrect: He **never** <u>has been</u> out of the country.

ADVERBS OF MANNER

With adverbs of manner, if the sentence has only one verb, you can place the adverb at the start of the sentence, before the verb, or after the verb or verb phrase. All are correct! Note that it says after the verb **or verb phrase**. You cannot place the adverb between the verb and its direct object. So it can't go directly after the verb.

> Correct: **Carefully**, she <u>opened</u> the safe.
>
> Correct: She **carefully** <u>opened</u> the safe.
>
> Correct: She <u>opened</u> the safe **carefully**.
>
> Incorrect: She <u>opened</u> **carefully** the safe. (Cannot put an adverb between the verb "opened" and the direct object "safe.")

If you have more than one verb, then you put the adverb before or after the verb to describe only that verb. If you want to describe the entire clause, then it goes after the clause.

> Correct: Mary **secretly** <u>told</u> Alan to leave her house.
>
> Correct: Mary <u>told</u> Alan **secretly** to leave her house.

In both cases, "secretly" modifies tell. It went before or after only "tell," not "leave."

> Correct: Mary asked Alan <u>to leave her house</u> **secretly**.

Here "secretly" modifies the verb clause "to leave her house," so it must come after the entire clause.

If you have an auxiliary verb, the adverb goes in between the auxiliary verb and main verb.

> Correct: She <u>couldn't</u> **calmly** <u>open</u> the safe.
>
> Incorrect: She **calmly** <u>couldn't open</u> the safe.
>
> Incorrect: She <u>couldn't open</u> **calmly** the safe.

Self-editing in practice

Original:

During her internship, Olivia only wrote two emails. In the first message, nervously she introduced herself to the marketing team, unsure if she belonged there. In the second, she reviewed the campaign plans carefully and suggested improvements that surprised the department head.

Yet those emails got the new manager's attention. She praised Olivia, who had just transferred from a different branch, in front of everyone. She was proud but unsure how to respond to the unexpected attention. Hoping to build on her success, the team was given a more ambitious project.

This project included a tight deadline. Their manager usually is calm during these high-pressure moments, but she told Olivia she needed to train the team. They gathered in the conference room on Tuesday, which had just been repainted. Olivia had carefully prepared her presentation slides and practiced them in the mirror. She delivered them confidently to the whole group.

Although just a temporary intern, the new team leader gave Olivia a key role in the next phase. She sometimes struggled with imposter syndrome, but her efforts were often appreciated. The email about the client feedback was sent before she left work by her supervisor. It praised her contributions and offered to write a letter of recommendation (generated by ChatGPT).

PAUSE HERE

Open your personalized workbook and correct any misplaced modifiers, then check my revision for the answers.

Revised:

> During her internship, Olivia wrote **only** two emails. In the first message, she **nervously** introduced herself to the marketing team, unsure if she belonged there. In the second, she reviewed the campaign plans carefully and suggested improvements that surprised the department head.
>
> Yet those emails got the new manager's attention. She praised Olivia, who had just transferred from a different branch, in front of everyone. She was proud but unsure how to respond to the unexpected attention. Hoping to build on her success, **Olivia was excited** when the team was given a more ambitious project.
>
> This project included a tight deadline. Their manager is **usually** calm during these high-pressure moments, but she told Olivia she needed to train the team. **On Tuesday**, they gathered in the conference room, **which had just been repainted**. Olivia had carefully prepared her presentation slides and practiced them in the mirror. She delivered them confidently to the whole group.
>
> Although just a temporary intern, **Olivia was given** a key role in the next phase. She sometimes struggled with imposter syndrome, but her efforts were often appreciated. **Before Olivia** left for work, an email with the client feedback was sent **by her supervisor**. It praised her contributions and offered to write a letter of recommendation.

I moved each modifier next to the word it modifies and added the ones that were missing. I would normally rewrite the second-to-last sentence to eliminate the passive voice, but I left it as is so I could focus solely on modeling misplaced modifiers.

EDITING STEPS

❏ Pause anytime a sentence feels confusing (when you can't easily tell what's being described or who's doing what). That confusion often signifies a misplaced modifier.

❏ Identify the modifier (descriptive words, phrases, or clauses) and ask, "Is this modifier next to what it describes?" Move it if not.

❏ Check for adverbs of frequency.

- Place them before the main verb
- Place them after forms of "to be"
- Place between auxiliary verb and main verb

❏ Check for adverbs of manner.

- Place them before or after the main verb
- Ensure they aren't separating a verb from its direct object

Verify Source Attributions

Plagiarism isn't always intentional. Some of the most expensive lawsuits in publishing history came from authors who genuinely didn't realize they needed to cite a paraphrased idea or attribute a statistic properly.

Don't be like them. Before you hand your manuscript to an editor, gather identifying information for every source you reference. Many editors (myself included!) can create your citations, but only *if* you've given us information to identify the source. In this stage, you need to note what needs a citation and collect at least one identifying detail for each source.[13] These include:

- URL
- Title of the book, article, podcast, etc.
- Author name

You at least need these details, but the more information you gather now, the less work (and cost) you'll face later.

When to cite?

To avoid plagiarism, you must cite your sources. Plagiarism can be intentional, such as copying a paragraph from a website without citation. But it can also be unintentional, like paraphrasing too closely or forgetting to cite a source.

---

13 Portions of this topic were drafted with AI assistance, then I edited and reviewed the output.

Plagiarism includes:

- Copying exact wording from a source without quotation marks or a citation (in some cases, you also need permission from the original author)
- Paraphrasing a source's idea or structure without credit
- Presenting another person's original insight as your own
- Using media (like photos, charts, or AI-generated graphics) without proper attribution

DIRECT QUOTES

If you quote someone directly, use quotation marks (or block formatting) and include a citation. This applies whether you're quoting a famous speech or a line from a blog post. When the words belong to someone else, you must give them credit.

Quotation marks:

> "If you quote someone directly, use quotation marks (or block formatting) and include a citation. This applies whether you're quoting a famous speech or a line from a blog post. When the words belong to someone else, you must give them credit" (*Self-Editing Essentials for Nonfiction*).

Block formatting:

> If you quote someone directly, use quotation marks (or block formatting) and include a citation. This applies whether you're quoting a famous speech or a line from a blog post. When the words belong to someone else, you must give them credit. (Katie Chambers)

Notice that block quotes don't need quotation marks, but they still require a citation.

> **Side note**
>
> I used block formatting throughout to indicate examples, not to indicate quotes. Block formatting can be used for other things, but when using it for a direct quote, you include the citation.

PARAPHRASED IDEAS

If you learned an idea from a source—even when you put it into your own words—you still need to cite it unless it's common knowledge, such as water freezes at 32 degrees Fahrenheit or most people need around eight hours of sleep.

Original quote:

> "People tend to retain more when they read physical books than e-books."

Paraphrase:

> Studies suggest people may retain more information from physical books than from digital formats.

> *That paraphrase will still need a citation, especially because it even follows the same syntax as the original.*

STATISTICS AND DATA

Numbers almost always require citation unless you gathered the data yourself through a survey or direct research.

> Eighty-one percent of Americans own a smartphone.

> According to Pew Research, 81 percent of Americans own a smartphone.

Both of these require a citation. Yes, you identified Pew Research in the second one, but that is only part of the citation. Note where you found it so your editor can create the citation or create the full citation yourself.

IMAGES, TABLES, CHARTS

Visuals sometimes need attribution, too, so always check the licensing.

If the image or graphic is in the public domain or released under a Creative Commons Zero (CCO) license, you typically don't need to cite it.

As for other Creative Commons licenses, check the details, as some require credit and others don't.

If you pay for an image, then you definitely need to give it credit. Free images often include restrictions on commercial use. You can use one on your website, for example, but need to purchase a license or provide proper attribution if you include it in a published book.

That said, it never hurts to credit the creator. If I used any image, table, or chart in a published work, regardless of licensing, I'd at least credit the creator. You may not need a full citation, but generally, you should acknowledge the creator.

What needs to go in a citation?

If you'd like to create your citations yourself, CMoS style is the standard in US mainstream books. If you're familiar with a different citation style, your editor can convert them.

Let's pretend we need to cite the book *The Managed Heart: Commercialization of Human Feeling* by Arlie Hochschild.

Citing Arlie's book looks a bit different in each format.

> CMoS footnote: Arlie Russell Hochschild, *The Managed Heart: Commercialization of Human Feeling* (Berkeley, California: University of California Press, 1983), 7.

> *APA: Hochschild, A. R. (1983). The managed heart: Commercialization of human feeling.* University of California Press.

> *MLA: Hochschild, Arlie Russell. The Managed Heart: Commercialization of Human Feeling.* Berkeley, California, University of California Press, 1983.

But while the format changes, the necessary information is often the same. So even if you're letting your editor handle the full citation, gather as much of the following as you can:

- Author(s) name
- Title of the work (book, article, blog post, video, etc.)
- Date of publication
- Publisher or website name
- URL (for online sources)
- Page number (for print sources, if quoting)

Some citation styles may ask for additional info like access dates or DOIs (digital object identifier, which is the gold standard for citing academic and scholarly work). Just keep in mind: the more details you gather up front, the easier the citation will be later.

Types of citations

If you don't feel comfortable creating citations, ask your editor to do it. But it's helpful to know which type you want.

IN-TEXT CITATIONS

This is the most common method in academic and journalistic writing.

A brief parenthetical reference appears right in the sentence or paragraph with the full citation information given in a works cited/bibliography at the end.

> In-text: "Climate change has accelerated in recent decades (NASA)."

> Bibliography entry: NASA. Climate Change: Vital Signs of the Planet. Accessed January 10, 2025. https://climate.nasa.gov.

In-text citations are concise, but can interrupt the flow in creative or narrative nonfiction. I don't suggest using them for non-academic books. The casual reader often sees them as "too academic." For self-help, how-to, general information, or a business book, I wouldn't use this type.

FOOTNOTES

A small superscript number appears after the cited content, with the full citation at the bottom of the page.

> "He coined the term 'emotional labor' to describe workplace empathy."[1]

> Full citation at bottom of page: 1 Arlie Russell Hochschild, *The Managed Heart: Commercialization of Human Feeling (Berkeley: University of California Press, 1983), 7.*

Footnotes are great for books because they let you give credit without breaking the narrative flow. They also allow space for commentary or extra info.

ENDNOTES

These work like footnotes, but all notes appear at the end of a chapter or book rather than at the bottom of the page. This keeps the page clean but makes referencing slower for the reader. This also works great for books. It just depends on whether you want to avoid page clutter or not.

EDITING STEPS

❑ Identify where you've quoted, paraphrased, or included data.

❑ Add a source note (example: URL, author name, title) after directly quoted or paraphrased ideas, and make sure to gather the identifying information.

❑ Gather full details for each source if you'd like.

❑ If you want to create citations, use a citation generator to help you if needed.

❑ Determine which citation style you want to use.

Yes, it's better to gather the source information before or during the drafting stage. But many don't. Many don't even do it before they come to me, so I'm including that step in this self-editing guide so you can at least make sure you've taken care of it before sending your manuscript to an editor.

If you haven't yet, scan the QR code or visit https://beaconpointservices.org/nonfiction-editing-workbook to generate your personalized workbook for the technical pass.

FEEDBACK PASS

You open your critique partner's notes and immediately think, *They didn't get it.* Five minutes later, you realize . . . they either nailed it or completely missed the point. You don't have to agree with every comment, but you should at least consider each one.

In the nonfiction space, critique partners are less common, but they do exist.

Critique Partner: Gives you more in-depth feedback as a writer in exchange for you doing the same for them.

Beta Readers: Give you feedback as a reader. They may also be writers, but in this role, they're responding as readers.

Do you need critique partners and/or beta readers?

The feedback pass helps you get a reader's perspective; something you can never have as the author. What makes sense to you may not make sense to a reader, so it's in your best interest to get feedback from others to get your manuscript in the best shape possible before enlisting an editor. Of course, you don't have to use either. However, the stronger your manuscript is before you send it to an editor, the less time (and money) you'll spend, and the better the final product will be.

As mentioned, critique partners are less common in nonfiction, but I recommend getting beta readers—people who represent your intended audience.

How to find good ones

That's out of the scope of this book, but check out *Finding the Write Fit* by Ross Lampert, which guides you in finding good critique partners and beta readers.

After that, you can read his entire Craft & Critique book series, which starts with *Giving and Receiving Effective Critique.* (Find the link to these and other resources in appendix B.)

Applying their feedback

Wait until you've received feedback from all your readers before implementing any of it. Yes, people will finish at different times, but resist the temptation to revise until you've gathered all the feedback.

ORGANIZE

First, compile all the feedback in one place: a Word document, Excel spreadsheet, notes app, etc.

Once compiled, group similar comments together. Create categories like feedback on specific chapters, particular concepts, overall impressions, writing style, etc.

Grouping makes it easier to spot common themes. If multiple readers flag the same chapter or concept, that's a clear sign something isn't working and deserves closer attention.

EVALUATE AND FILTER

With everything grouped by category (organization, content, writing style, chapter 5, etc.), decide which comments truly don't fit your vision and set them aside. If it's a common theme, pause and ask whether it's your ego or favoritism talking. You may love a specific section, but if several readers struggle with it, pay attention.

Ultimately, you decide what to implement and what to ignore. My only advice is to give real consideration to each piece of feedback without letting your ego interfere. Ask whether the suggestion would genuinely strengthen the manuscript.

You aren't going to please everyone, so don't take every opinion to heart. Remove the feedback that doesn't resonate or serve your vision, and keep the rest.

PRIORITIZE

Once you've filtered the list, tackle the big-picture feedback first and save the smaller details for later. For instance, if readers feel confused by a concept in chapter three, fix that before worrying about smoothing out transition sentences.

You may find it helpful not only to list what you'll tackle first, but also to arrange those items in manuscript order. For example, address big-picture feedback for chapter one before tackling big-picture feedback for chapter six.

DIVE IN

Now work through your list and make the changes. Trust your judgment, stay open to improvement, and remember, this feedback is helping you create the strongest version of your book. Once you've implemented the feedback that serves your vision, you'll have a manuscript that's reader-tested and ready for the next stage: professional editing.

OTHER FEEDBACK

Certain topics may benefit from feedback from a sensitivity reader—someone with lived experience in a particular area who reviews your manuscript for potentially harmful, inaccurate, or stereotypical representations. Their goal is to help you avoid unintentional harm.

If your book deals with mental health conditions, trauma and abuse, disability and chronic illness, cultural or religious topics outside your experience, LGBTQ+ experiences, and different races and ethnicities, then get a sensitivity check.

Keep in mind that one sensitivity reader doesn't represent an entire community. If you're writing about a complex topic, consider hiring multiple sensitivity readers when your budget allows. Each person's lived experience matters, but perspectives within any group vary widely.

EDITING STEPS

- ❑ Compile all feedback in one place.
- ❑ Group similar comments together by category:
  - Chapters
  - Concepts
  - Overall impressions
  - Writing style
  - Other themes
- ❑ Identify common themes.
- ❑ Review feedback category by category and remove any that don't resonate or serve your vision. (Pause and reflect on feedback and consider first if it's valid.)
- ❑ Create an editing checklist, addressing big-picture feedback first (concepts, structure), then handling smaller details (transitions, phrasing, word choice).
  - ○ Optional: arrange feedback in manuscript order.
- ❑ Work through prioritized feedback one item at a time.

CONCLUSION

Whew! You made it.

If you feel overwhelmed by the self-editing process, I get it. While writing a book is brave, self-editing one is braver. I've heard from many authors that editing took them longer than the actual writing. And they're not alone. Many famous authors have said some version of "good writing is rewriting!" No one's unedited draft comes out brilliant. None of them.

If you've made it this far, you've proven you're committed not just to finishing a manuscript but to becoming a stronger, more thoughtful writer. So just remember to take it slowly, and don't try to edit for everything. Two or three topics per pass are enough. Then incorporate feedback from your beta readers and get your manuscript off to an editor.

I hope these techniques and the tools I talked about, plus those listed in appendices A and B, stay with you long after you close this book. That way, when you sit down to self-edit your next book, you'll already have a process—and a partner in these pages—to guide you.

Keep going. Your message matters, and the world needs the light only you can offer. So use my free gift to you (see the next page) to publish your book so the world can hear from you.

Keep shining your beacon brightly,

Katie Chambers

GIFT FOR YOU
The Professional Editing Roadmap

You did it! You self-edited your whole manuscript. Take a second and enjoy that. If that superhuman pose, piece of pie, or dancing that you did before you self-edited worked, do it again. Or take your celebration to the next level: throw on the most amazing outfit in your closet, cue up your favorite song, and dance in every room in your house, or perform a victory lap around your entire neighborhood, screaming "I'm amazing."

After the celebration, it's time for the next step: professional editing. That might sound easy: find an editor, hand off your draft, and relax.

But

- Do you know how to find the right editor for your book?
- Do you know what red and green flags to look for and what questions to ask before hiring them?
- Once the edits come back, are you ready for markup you didn't expect?
- Do you know how to revise and rewrite based on external feedback?
- Do you know how much time and money to budget for and how to work on a limited budget?

If you answered yes to all of those, great! But if you'd like some help, I've got you.

I'm offering a free gift to all authors who picked up this book— The Professional Editing Roadmap: 6 Steps to Hiring the Right Editor, Navigating the Editing Process, and Getting the Most From Your Investment.

This free six-step email course gives you everything you need to go into the editing process informed and confident:

- **Step 1: What to Expect When Working with an Editor.** This debunks 10 common false assumptions about editing and replaces them with realistic expectations, so you know exactly what the author-editor relationship will look like from the start.
- **Step 2: Inside the Editor's Studio.** This breaks down the four levels of editing so you know exactly what your book needs (and what you'll be hiring and paying for).
- **Step 3: How Much Will This Be Again?** This is where I'll break down why editing costs what it does, a workable budget, and some smart strategies when you're in a rush or money is tight.
- **Step 4: From Start to Finish.** This lays out the entire editing process ahead of time so you can have a bird's-eye view of what happens from first search to final returned edits.
- **Step 5: Responding, Revising, and Rewriting.** This digs into dealing with Tracked Changes, making informed choices based on editor's suggestions, and even pushing back when you disagree (it will happen, and it's okay when it does!).
- **Step 6: The Right Editor for Me.** This brings everything together to help you understand exactly who you're looking for to make *your* book the best it can be (and what it looks like when you find them!).

This email course will teach you everything you need to know to find, hire, and work with not just any editor, but the perfect one for your book.

Not every editor will walk you through all of that. This course will.

Sign up free at https://beaconpointservices.org/get-free-resource/ or scan the QR code below.

Reader Bonus: 50% off the Author Management Tracker

(NORMALLY $29 — YOUR PRICE: $14.50)

The Author Management Tracker gives you a single, organized system to manage your journey.

Built in Excel, it replaces scattered notes and multiple homemade spreadsheets with one clear place to track your progress, deadlines, and budget as you move through editing, publishing, and launch—so you're not constantly wondering what's next or what you might be forgetting.

Get access to your free Professional Editing Roadmap and your reader-only discount by scanning the QR code or visiting https://beaconpointservices.org/get-free-resource/.

Now You Get the Red Pen

Share your feedback by reviewing on Amazon and/or Goodreads.

Any review—good, neutral, or "Katie, what were you thinking?"—helps other readers decide if this book is right for them.

Just a few honest sentences can help a future reader decide whether to invest their time and money.

If I survived 8th graders, I can survive honest feedback. So tell it straight.

I'll just be over here, refreshing my dashboard and appreciating you more than you know.

AMAZON

GOODREADS

ABOUT THE AUTHOR

Katie Chambers is a developmental editor and copyeditor and the owner of Beacon Point LLC, where she helps nonfiction authors clarify their message and organize their ideas with purpose and polish. Her specialty is reorganizing nonfiction manuscripts so they flow logically and powerfully—guiding readers from first page to final takeaway without confusion or overwhelm.

As a former middle and high school English teacher with specialized training in writing instruction, Katie brings a teacher's heart to every edit. She's a hands-on editor who models clarity in the text and explains the reasoning behind revisions, helping authors better understand the editing process and make smarter choices in future drafts.

When she's not editing, you'll find her reading, eating out, snuggling with her cats, cooking, or hanging out with her supportive husband and their three kids.

Learn more and explore free resources at beaconpointservices.org.

APPENDIX A

Beacon Point Resources

If you're unsure what topics you should edit for or how to apply them to your manuscript, I have two options to help you with more guided self-editing.

Manuscript Checkup service

I charge a flat $500 for this bridge service. This service is for authors who want professional feedback to help guide their self-editing and save time and money before getting full editing or submitting to an agent.

I will

- professionally edit your first 10k words
- provide a detailed letter on what's working and where you need to focus your editing attention
- provide a one-on-one coaching call, teaching you how to edit for specific craft techniques your manuscript needs, walking you through my thinking process and how I go about making edits in your manuscript (since I will have only seen the first 10k words, I can't assess the top two in each pass. I can only go off the 10k words to determine the greatest needs. If granted permission, I can run your manuscript through my custom diagnostic AI tool explained below, then use the rubric to help guide the coaching call)

- provide feedback for one self-revised chapter after the coaching call, so you know you're applying the techniques well

Self-Editing Diagnostic tool

This tool is being designed (will be coming out in 2026) to help authors identify their top revision priorities by analyzing patterns across an entire manuscript and mapping them to the editing topics covered in this book.

The goal is not to replace editorial judgment or hands-on revision, but to help you focus your time and energy where it will make the biggest difference and to offer individualized guidance on how to apply self-editing techniques more effectively in relation to your manuscript.

HOW IT'S INTENDED TO WORK

When available, the diagnostic tool will:

Highlight editing priorities. Using a rubric aligned with this guide—along with clearly defined analysis questions, clear indicators of strengths, and common weak flags (I wrote all of them)—the tool will identify which editing topics are most likely to need attention in your manuscript.

Provide a clear scorecard. Rather than vague feedback, the tool will offer a structured overview showing which areas appear strong and which would benefit from focused revision in each pass.

Illustrate issues with examples. Where helpful, the tool will surface short excerpts from your manuscript to illustrate specific craft issues for each lower-scoring topic in each pass. These examples are meant to support learning, not to overwrite your voice or dictate revisions.

A NOTE ABOUT AI AND ANALYSIS

Although this tool uses AI as the customer-facing interface to present results clearly and in plain language, AI is not acting as the editor. The analysis itself is based on structured criteria drawn from this guide, with my editorial oversight and coding. The underlying system evaluates patterns and indicators in your manuscript, while AI is used to explain the results and reasoning in a clear, readable way.

Think of AI here as the messenger, not the decision-maker.

PRIVACY PROTECTION

Your manuscript remains your intellectual property, and protecting it is central to how this tool is being designed.

- Your full manuscript is not reviewed by a conversational, chat-based AI. It *will not see* your manuscript. While you upload your file through an AI-based interface, the manuscript itself is processed by a separate off-site diagnostic system designed specifically for this analysis.
- Only short excerpts may be reviewed by AI, and only when necessary to explain a specific craft issue. These excerpts are kept to a minimum.
- Your writing is not used to train AI models. Your content is not added to any dataset or reused in any way.
- Files are stored only as long as needed to generate your report or resolve technical issues.

Visit https://beaconpointservices.org/author-products/#diagnostic to sign up to be notified when the tool is ready or scan the QR code.

I've finished self-editing, now what?

Congratulations! You've strengthened your manuscript and grown as a writer.

If you're ready to hire an editor, I'd love for you to consider my team and me. You need to feel good about the editor you go with, and we're not the right editor for everyone. So, do reach out to a few editors to determine the best fit for you.

> We offer a sample edit and/or discovery call to determine if we're the right fit. Just go to scan the QR code or visit https://beaconpointservices.org/editing-nonfiction-authors/ and fill out a request form. 

Genres Beacon Point edits

- Business books
- Self-help/how-to
- Religious guidebooks (Christian and alternative spirituality)
- Memoir
- General information books

I can refer you to an editor if you have an academic, medical, scientific, legal, or philosophy/theory-heavy book, textbook, or technical manual. Just email me.

Rates & Services

*These are my rates at the time of publishing this book. If my rates have increased, just mention you read this book, and I'll honor these rates.

Substantive/Developmental Editing, $0.035–$0.055 per word: Deals with organization and content issues

Copyediting, $0.027–$0.04 per word: Deals with word- and sentence-level issues (writing-pass and technical-pass concepts)

Combined Package, $0.04–$0.07 per word: Combines both types of editing in one round for a discounted rate to meet authors' budgetary constraints

Manuscript Checkup, $500: A bridge service for authors who want professional feedback to help guide their self-editing and save time and money before getting full editing or submitting to an agent.

APPENDIX B

Additional Resources for You

Being an author, especially a self-published one, involves a lot. So, to help you through the process, I have curated resources for you. You can also check out the resource center on my website, which mentions all the ones below plus my free blogs, webinars, and courses; recommended service providers; and more. https://beaconpointservices.org/writing-resources/.

If you're going the traditional route, several resources still apply to you, though some are specific to self-publishing.

I've grouped the resources by topic:

- Assisted self-publishing companies
- Networking and learning
- Grammar, punctuation, and spelling help
- Feedback pass help
- Marketing help
- Audiobook narration
- Author business and publishing

ASSISTED SELF-PUBLISHING COMPANIES

You need to be careful to avoid assisted self-publishing scams. Unfortunately, a lot of bad actors are masquerading as hybrid publishers, and they take your money and don't do much for you. I've personally vetted all these companies; of course, you can find plenty of other good ones.

JWC Publishing: https://www.jacobswc.com

Precocity Press: https://www.precocitypress.com

Bedside Reading: https://www.bedsidereading.com/
publishing.html

SWATT Books: https://swatt-books.co.uk

Archangel Ink: http://bit.ly/2FrrXuB (my affiliate link)

Stellar Houston Communications: https://stellarwriter.com/
publishing

Jennifer Wilkov's Done-For-You Publishing: https://
yourbookisyourhook.com/services/collaborative-services/
book-done-for-you

Ghostwriters Network Publishing: https://ghostwritersnetwork
.com/get-published

Credible Ink: https://www.credible.ink/

NETWORKING AND LEARNING

Each of these communities includes networking and learning opportunities.

Alliance of Independent Authors ($119 a year): They "campaign for author rights and offer tailored education, trusted resources, and a global community so you can publish and sell with confidence."

https://www.allianceindependentauthors.org/members/
join?affid=21111 (my affiliate link)

Biz Book Pub Hub (free community): "Through the Hub, you are one degree away from any author resource you know you need. . . [They're] building an engaged community of writers and authors, specifically entrepreneurs writing books to grow their business." Join their free networking events and get access to all the Hub Partners.

> https://robbiesamuels.com/hub

Authors Collaborative Membership Community ($997 a year or $97 monthly): Get access to a community to network with others, step-by-step processes, live support calls, and marketing support.

> https://www.getcontentconfident.com/a/2147511494/LiHjiY8G
> (my affiliate link)

> Smart Author System (£497 or £797): If you haven't written your book yet, this program will take you all the way from drafting to writing to publishing and marketing. You can do the self-study version, which is the £497 price, or the community version.

> https://b4g0qhvnucmxo.krtra.com/t/yFlfvtWgPdZa
> (my affiliate link)

Twin Flame Studios (free): They host live expert panels and Q&A sessions covering every topic imaginable in the industry. You can register for these free panels on their website. Just go to "Live Events." They also have a directory of curated industry professionals (go to "Author Resources").

> https://twinflamesstudios.com/audiobook-services/?nowprocket=
> 1partnerid=r1675 (my partner link)

Nonfiction Authors Association (plans from $39 a month to $665 a quarter): Founded by Stephanie Chandler, the Nonfiction Authors Association is a community and resource hub built specifically for non-fiction writers. From marketing strategies and platform building to their annual online writers conference, it's a supportive space designed to help nonfiction authors publish and promote their books with confidence.

https://nonfictionauthorsassociation.com/join/

GRAMMAR, PUNCTUATION, AND SPELLING HELP

Given the wide range of this topic, I didn't cover these topics in depth. If you're interested in expanding your learning, check out these resources.

Tricky Quickies Series by Debbie Emmitt (£5.99–7.99): These books "clearly and concisely explain similar, everyday English words and phrases, with handy examples of use."

https://www.debbie-emmitt.com/books-and-resources/
tricky-quickies

Grammar Girl (free): She "provides short, friendly tips to improve your writing and feed your love of the English language."

https://www.quickanddirtytips.com/grammar-girl

Grammar Conundrums Course by Catherine Turner ($27): "Grammar Conundrums includes tons of example sentences so you can see these tricky words in action AND 750 quiz questions to help you lock in that knowledge forever."

https://turnerproofreading.com/grammar-conundrums

Punctuation 101 eBook and Workbook by Catherine Turner ($17): "An ebook and workbook combo that'll help you refresh your memory of punctuation rules, learn the punctuation mistakes you need to avoid making, and polish your punctuation skills so you can wow your readers."

https://turnerproofreading.com/punctuation-101

FEEDBACK PASS HELP

Learn how to receive and give effective critique from the Critique Doctor, Ross Lampert.

Finding the Write Fit: The Critique Doctor's guide to finding the critique partnership that works for you (Craft & Critique Book 0)

https://books2read.com/u/mYO8wY

Giving and Receiving Effective Critique: The Critique Doctor's guide to helping other writers write better (and still be your friends) (Craft & Critique Book 1)

https://books2read.com/u/49Grld

Mechanics, Narrative, and Description: The Critique Doctor's guide to helping other writers (and yourself) create clear, compelling prose (Craft & Critique Book 2)

https://books2read.com/u/4NOogJ

MARKETING

This is often the hardest yet most important step for authors to learn. Check out these resources to help you.

Book Marketing Webinar by Teddy Smith and Aryn Van Dyke (free): It covers how to master your book launch, leverage AI to supercharge your Amazon ads, engage your audience and build buzz, and learn how other authors transformed their sales using these methods.

https://www.youtube.com/watch?v=5HsijrfNRgg

***Launch Your Book: An Entrepreneur's Guide to Reviews that Drive Revenue* by Robbie Samuels ($0.99–$15.99):** Award-winning author and book launch strategist Robbie Samuels shares the proven approach he's used to coach entrepreneurs through launching a nonfiction book, attracting Amazon reviews, and turning their book into a pipeline for business growth.

https://linktr.ee/LAUNCH_Your_Book

Book Sirens ($10 one-time fee plus $2 per reader OR $100 a year for multiple books): Find ARC readers from their 51,000+ book reviewers and influencers and grow your mailing list.

https://booksirens.com/?affiliate=DTX0NV8 (my affiliate link)

Booksprout (plans ranging from $9 to $29 a month): Find ARC readers from their 90,000 active reviewers.

https://booksprout.co/?ref=katie-chambers38 (my affiliate link, which gets you a free month)

Book PR Checklist by Bianca Sanders (free): This is a cheat sheet to book PR to get you started on your marketing journey.

https://www.myrtileditorial.com/bookprchecklist

Improve Your Author Website by Debbie Emmitt (£9.95): This guide will help you improve your author website to attract readers and agents, move up in search results, and look polished and professional.

https://www.debbie-emmitt.com/improve-your-author-website

Author Marketing & Launch Notion Planner by Shelly Zevlever (CAD $6.99): This Notion page is set up to accompany you across the process of setting up your social media accounts, getting ready for launch, and all the details in between that help you market your book.

https://shellyzev.com/author-marketing-and-launch

Book Award Pro (plans ranging from free to $69 a month): They operate the world's largest database of legitimate reviews and awards and match you up with the awards that are right for your book.

https://bookawardpro.com

David Gaughran's newsletter. Sign up for his valuable marketing newsletter and get a free marketing book and course.

https://davidgaughran.com/following-free-newsletter/

AUDIOBOOK NARRATION

If your book lends itself well to audiobook format, you're leaving money on the table but not looking into it.

Narrate Your Own Book minicourse by professional actor David H. Lawrence XVII (free): This free minicourse will help you understand how to become the voice of your own audiobook.

https://narrateyourownbook.com

Narrate Your Own Book Course by professional actor David H. Lawrence XVII ($1,995 or three monthly payments of $697): The course walks you through preparing your manuscript for audiobook format, creating your home studio equipment (he provides the equipment), learning voice acting skills, handling the production workflow, and releasing and marketing your new audiobook.

https://go.narrateyourownbook.com/referral/nyob/
euVYnrsalHmxICog (my affiliate link)

Connect with an Audience of Millions Using the Power of Your Audiobook by Tina Dietz of Twin Flame Studios (free): Learn tips to make the audiobook process easier and what options can save you time and money. Plus, learn how to turn your audiobook into content that drives more book and audio sales.

https://twinflamesstudios.com/connect/?partnerid=r1675
(my affiliate link)

Audiobook production services by Twin Flames Studio: They will do the editing, mastering, proofing, distributing, and marketing for your audiobook. They offer two options: author as narrator (they provide remote support and direction on performance and tech) or professional as narrator (they have a network of 7,000+)

> https://twinflamesstudios.com/audiobook-services/?nowprocket
> =1partnerid=r1675 (my affiliate link)

AUTHOR BUSINESS AND PUBLISHING

The Creative Penn: Run by bestselling author Joanna Penn, this site is a go-to hub for authors who want to think beyond the manuscript and build a sustainable writing career. She covers everything from self-publishing and book marketing to AI tools and direct sales, and her long-running podcast is one of the most comprehensive in the industry.

> https://www.thecreativepenn.com/

Jane Friedman: Jane Friedman is one of the most trusted voices in publishing, with deep experience in both traditional and indie paths. Her site offers authoritative guidance on book proposals, query letters, publishing options, and the business of being an author — an essential bookmark for any nonfiction writer navigating the industry.

> https://janefriedman.com/

APPENDIX C

Master Self-Editing Checklist

If you want a printable master list, you can go to https://beaconpointservices.org/nonfiction -editing-workbook and download the PDF master list.

Content Pass

Create an effective introduction

- ❏ Mark each key element in your introduction (hook, promise value, provide credibility, roadmap) and add in any you're missing.
- ❏ Revise if your chapter overview contains a chapter-by-chapter, topic-by-topic breakdown.
- ❏ Add in your voice and personality where applicable.
- ❏ Delete any content that veers into overexplaining territory.

Strengthen chapter hooks

- ❏ Pause at the end of the first paragraph or first few paragraphs of every chapter and ask if you have an engaging hook. If not, revise.
- ❏ Identify the hook types you use and make sure not to use the same type in every chapter.

Delete unnecessary repetition

❏ Highlight phrases, concepts, or anecdotes that appear frequently.

❏ Look at what you have highlighted and delete any redundant and unnecessary content, rephrase any necessary content for reinforcement, or merge it with earlier content discussing the same concept.

Add necessary information

❏ Pause anytime you're describing a new concept and ask these questions. If you answer no to the first two or yes to the others, add in the necessary details.

- Have you defined it clearly and given strong, concrete examples, answering all the "but whys" the reader needs to know?
- Have you assumed prior knowledge that your reader may not have?
- Have you explained how content relates to each other rather than leaping from one idea to the other?
- Do you have any terms, acronyms, or industry jargon that your target reader may stumble over?
- Could a visual aid (table, checklist, step-by-step summary) help clarify your point?

❏ Pause anytime you have a personal story and ask if this story is balanced with actionable takeaways? (Do include your own experiences—just ensure they serve the reader, not your ego.) If not, make sure to include the takeaway from the story unless it's implied. You don't want to insult the reader by stating the obvious.

❏ At the end of each chapter, ask these questions. If the answer is no, add in the necessary details.

- Did you deliver on the promise of this chapter?
- Does this chapter offer practical insights (a clear how), and original thinking, not just theory or surface-level advice (unless you intended for this chapter to be theoretical, but you shouldn't have too many of those)?

Ensure reader-friendly content

❑ If you don't have any stories (yours, others', or made-up ones), add some in. Make sure to connect them back to the reader so they serve a point.

❑ Define any necessary jargon.

❑ Rewrite any sentence or section that is reminiscent of an English essay.

❑ If you use "I" too often, rewrite to use more "you" and "we."

❑ Switch from "we" to "you" when giving action steps or lessons.

❑ Provide exercises, action steps, and/or questions for them to answer if it makes sense for your book.

Align genre and audience expectations

❑ Change any writing that doesn't match the tone of your genre.

❑ Add in any necessary genre expectations you're missing.

    ○ (Note: You don't necessarily need all genre expectations. For example, some how-to books don't lend themselves to visuals, so you wouldn't need to include them. You do want to include most, if not all, the expectations.)

❑ Rewrite or change the genre if your book doesn't fulfill the genre promise.

❑ Rewrite any passages that don't meet the tone for the genre.

❑ Look for opportunities to speak directly to your target audience and address their specific needs.

❑ Trim or delete information your target audience already knows so the content stays focused and engaging.

❑ Revise or delete any sections that feel off-genre or too advanced/basic for your audience.

Organization Pass

Ensure logical order

- ❑ Examine each chapter in context and ask, "Does this chapter belong in this spot? Is it thematically grouped or part of a natural sequence?" If not, and multiple aren't, figure out whether to group them by theme or progression and reorganize them.
- ❑ Examine each chapter in context and ask, "Would the transition work better between these chapters if the order was switched?" If so, then flip the chapter order.
- ❑ Check that every paragraph aligns with the chapter's overall topic. Flag it if it doesn't.
- ❑ Check that all content under a given heading relates to that heading's focus. Flag it if it doesn't.
- ❑ Review all headings within a chapter and ask if each one is in the right spot progressively or thematically. Flag any misplaced headings.
- ❑ Review all flagged items and delete anything redundant or off topic, or move it to a more fitting chapter or section.

Refine headings and subheadings

- ❑ Check for outlier chapters that either don't use headings or go deeper in nesting than others. If only one chapter breaks the pattern, revise it for consistency.
- ❑ Delete unnecessary headings and subheadings (especially those that separate short, related paragraphs that could easily flow together with a transition).
- ❑ Add in necessary headings to break up long stretches of text or to clarify major topic shifts.
- ❑ Nest heading levels logically, where subtopics clearly belong under a larger idea.

Strengthen or add transitions

- ❏ Pause whenever you switch to a new idea (Identify where your topic or focus shifts, even slightly.)
- ❏ Ask, "Does the transition contain a clear relationship between the ideas up front before readers get too deep into the new topic?"
- ❏ If not or if you don't even have a transition, write or rewrite one using the transition formula: Mention the old topic → introduce the new topic → show the connection.

Ensure effective paragraph breaks

- ❏ Highlight any paragraph that runs longer than 150–200 words (8–10 lines in your book format). Ask, Does this long paragraph contain multiple distinct ideas? If yes, look for natural breaking points where the focus shifts. If not, keep it as is.
- ❏ Check for variety: Do you have a mix of short, medium, and longer paragraphs, or are they all roughly the same length?
- ❏ Look for moments that deserve emphasis. Could a key statement land harder as a single-sentence paragraph?
- ❏ If you've included dialogue or conversations in your anecdotes, make sure you're breaking for each new speaker.
- ❏ Scan for areas with several short paragraphs in a row and ensure each paragraph is introducing a new idea rather than just breaking up a paragraph that was split only because it looked too long. Put paragraphs together that belong together.

Writing Pass

Ensure good sentence fluency

❏ Pause when a section sounds flat, repetitive, or monotonous. (Don't just look at one paragraph. Read across multiple to detect hidden rhythm issues.)

❏ Check the sentence beginnings: Do too many in a row follow the same sentence-beginning pattern even if the starting word varies?

❏ Check the sentence lengths and types: Are most of the sentences the same length? Do they follow the same type?

❏ Revise with intentional variety if you answered yes to any of the above questions.

Eliminate excess "to be" verbs

❏ Stop when a passage feels wordy, flat, or overly dependent on "be" verbs.

❏ Scan the section for an overuse of "be" verbs.

❏ Revise by reducing "be" verbs using any of the six strategies:
  - Swap for a stronger verb
  - Cut "be" verb and change –ing form of verb
  - Show instead of tell
  - Change another word in the sentence to the verb
  - Combine sentences
  - Rearrange sentence order
  - Get rid of unnecessary phrases

Reduce wordiness

❏ Stop when a sentence (even short sentences) feels like a mouthful and/or has several little words, and revise to avoid
  - qualifiers

- prep phrases
- nominalizations
- adjectivizations
- expletive constructions
- unnecessary "which" or "that"

❑ Combine sentences that use "this" as the beginning of the second one.

❑ Check for sentence pairs you can combine using a colon and –ing word or by trimming portions.

❑ Revise for conciseness without sacrificing meaning, tone, or clarity.

Maintain a consistent tone

❑ Review your intro and make sure it sets the tone you want to use throughout the book. If it does, note that tone.

❑ Read each chapter and check for mismatches in tone.

❑ Look for sections where the language becomes more formal, casual, academic, or emotional than the rest. Highlight any tone shifts that don't match the intended voice. Then revise accordingly.

Ensure accurate reading level

❑ Run a readability check on a few sample chapters to establish your baseline reading level.

❑ Compare your score to your target audience's needs (seventh to ninth grade for general nonfiction, higher for specialized audiences).

❑ If your score is too high, identify sections with:
- Long sentences (20+ words)
- Complex vocabulary
- Passive voice
- Abstract or formal phrasing

❑ Revise using these strategies:
- Break long sentences into shorter ones

- Replace complex words with simpler alternatives
- Convert passive voice to active voice
- Use concrete examples instead of abstract concepts
- Speak directly to the reader using "you"

❏ Run another readability check on revised sections to ensure improvement.

Technical Pass

❏ Run general find-and-replace tasks

Correct easily confused words

❏ Use Word's "find" feature to search for the first word in a pair you tend to confuse.

❏ Check whether each result is used correctly in context.

❏ Search for the second word in the pair and review its usage.

❏ Repeat with each word pair you struggle with.

Fix common comma errors

❏ Watch out for run-ons. Check all coordinating conjunctions (FANBOYS) between two clauses. If each side could stand alone as its own sentence, insert a comma before the FANBOYS. If one side is a phrase (not a full sentence), a comma usually isn't needed, though you can stylistically choose to have one.

❏ Watch out for comma splices. If two sentences are joined with just a comma, fix it by adding the missing FANBOYS or make it a period.

❏ Watch out for fused sentences. If two sentences are not joined by anything, fix it by using one of the correct methods (comma and FANBOYS, semicolon, colon) or split it into two sentences with a period.

❑ Look at sentences with introductory words, clauses, or phrases. If a sentence starts with something before the main subject-verb clause, check if it needs a comma.

❑ Check that commas are helping clarity, not cluttering the sentence. If you're using commas "just in case," double-check the rules to see where they're actually needed.

Correct unnecessary capitalization

❑ Check all capitalized words and change them to lowercase if
  - you capitalized them because they "felt important"
  - it's a job title that doesn't come before a name
  - it's a concept, framework, or step that isn't an official name
  - you're using caps for emphasis

❑ If you feel strongly about any of them, let your editor know because they will lowercase them otherwise.

Revise misplaced modifiers

❑ Pause anytime a sentence feels confusing (when you can't easily tell what's being described or who's doing what). That confusion often signifies a misplaced modifier.

❑ Identify the modifier (descriptive words, phrases, or clauses) and ask, "Is this modifier next to what it describes?" Move it if not.

❑ Check for adverbs of frequency.
  - Place them before the main verb
  - Place them after forms of "to be"
  - Place between auxiliary verb and main verb

❑ Check for adverbs of manner.
  - Place them before or after the main verb
  - Ensure they aren't separating a verb from its direct object

Verify source attribution

- ❑ Identify where you've quoted, paraphrased, or included data.
- ❑ Add a source note (example: URL, author name, title) after directly quoted or paraphrased ideas, and make sure to gather the identifying information.
- ❑ Gather full details for each source if you'd like.
- ❑ If you want to create the citations, use a citation generator to help you if needed.
- ❑ Determine which citation style you want to use.

Feedback Pass

- ❑ Compile all feedback in one place.
- ❑ Group similar comments together by category:
    - Chapters
    - Concepts
    - Overall impressions
    - Writing style
    - Other themes
- ❑ Identify common themes.
- ❑ Review feedback category by category and remove any that don't resonate or serve your vision. (Pause and reflect on feedback and consider first if it's valid.)
- ❑ Create an editing checklist, addressing big-picture feedback first (concepts, structure), then handling smaller details (transitions, phrasing, word choice).
    - ○ Optional: arrange feedback in the order it appears in the manuscript.
- ❑ Work through prioritized feedback one at a time.